PUSHKIN PRESS CLASSICS

⸻R PARIS

WARTIME NOTEBOOKS

'Clouds Over Paris *is the most fascinating account of how normal war can seem, how the most everyday issues seem more important than the biggest historical issues of the day'*
JEWISH CHRONICLE

'With gentle irony, Hartlaub depicts the institutionalised mendacity of the German occupiers, so wary of the wiles of the French, yet so easily seduced by the lies of their own bellicose propaganda'
THE CRITIC

FELIX HARTLAUB grew up in Mannheim, the son of an art historian and museum director who was ejected from his post by the Nazis in 1933 for his support of 'degenerate' art. Hartlaub studied history and was called up immediately upon graduating in 1939. Initially serving in a barrage balloon unit, he was sent to Paris in late 1940 to do archival research for the German foreign office, using his spare time to document the city in the notebooks that comprise *Clouds over Paris*. He would continue writing diaries throughout the war up until he went missing in Berlin in May 1945.

SIMON BEATTIE is an antiquarian bookseller, literary translator, and choral composer.

RÜDIGER GÖRNER is Professor of German with Comparative Literature at Queen Mary, University of London.

CLOUDS OVER PARIS

WARTIME NOTEBOOKS

FELIX HARTLAUB

TRANSLATED FROM THE GERMAN
BY SIMON BEATTIE

WITH AN INTRODUCTION
BY RÜDIGER GÖRNER

PUSHKIN PRESS CLASSICS

Pushkin Press
Somerset House, Strand
London WC2R ILA

First published by Pushkin Press in 2022
This edition published in 2023

1 3 5 7 9 8 6 4 2

ISBN 13: 978-1-78227-846-7

Designed and typeset by Tetragon, London
Printed and bound by Clays Ltd, Elcograf S.p.A.

www.pushkinpress.com

Contents

Introduction

The Unhappy Occupier

I

"On the meaning of diaries. They can only refer to a certain layer of occurrences that happen in the intellectual and physical sphere. What concerns us most intimately resists communication if not our very own perception of it." So wrote Ernst Jünger, the German officer and well-known writer of First World War memoirs, in his *Paris Diary* on 18th November 1941. Jünger wrote this about a year after the young unknown lance corporal Felix Hartlaub first prepared to be relocated to Paris, where he also would begin keeping a diary, one more impressionistic in style than that of literature's most famous Wehrmacht officer. The two men's paths could have easily crossed, though, on the German-occupied banks of the Seine or elsewhere. The one thing they shared was a sense of the surrealism of their situation, which the young soldier Hartlaub found oppressive. Jünger, the established author and high-ranking officer, was to receive a ticket from Jean Cocteau himself for a viewing of the surrealist film *Le sang d'un poète* ("The Blood of a Poet").

But who, then, was Felix Hartlaub (1913–1945)? A Francophile loner in German-occupied Paris, where he worked for the German Ministry of Foreign Affairs from December 1940 to August 1941 as a historian at the Quai d'Orsay. Later, in a letter to his father, he called it the "Cabinet du Sinistre". For after the French surrender to the Germans, the Quai d'Orsay appeared ghostlike, void of real life like most of occupied Paris, or so it seemed to Hartlaub, the diarist and detached observer, who was mostly embarrassed by his and his fellow Germans' presence in the then half-deserted metropolis on the Seine, the old capital of the nineteenth century.

Literary history was Hartlaub's vocation, but military history was his profession: he wrote his doctorate on the sea battle of Lepanto (1571) and the role of Don Juan d'Austria, a battle in which, incidentally, the future author of *Don Quixote*, Miguel de Cervantes, had fought, and in which he had lost the use of his left arm. In fact, this turned out to be Hartlaub's only publication during his short life. It was not by choice but sheer destiny that he eventually found himself in a small circle of historians in the closest vicinity of the *Führerhauptquartier* recording the events of the war, before he vanished without a trace in the last days of April 1945, during the pointless defence of Berlin against the Soviets.

Hartlaub was a highly educated aspiring young writer who produced only notes and fragments. In fact, when reading his literary texts, including his *Clouds over Paris*, now available for the first time in English, one has the distinct impression that they were intended to serve as material for novels to be written later. But there was also Hartlaub the writer of fine letters, largely to his father Gustav Friedrich Hartlaub, the eminent art historian and former director of the Kunsthalle Mannheim, which was, thanks to him, until 1933 one of the foremost exhibitors of avant-garde art in Germany. Vilified by the Nazis of Mannheim, he ended up forced to live the life of a private, demonstratively non-political scholar in nearby Heidelberg. He was able to afford this way of life thanks to his second marriage to the daughter of a wealthy industrialist following the premature death of his first wife and Felix's mother. During this time, Gustav was able to publish pieces on art history in the *Frankfurter Zeitung*, one of the few papers in Nazi Germany that managed to maintain some degree of independence from the official ideology. The art historian's preoccupation with mirrors in art was something he passed on to his son, who was to reflect in his diaries on the meaning of mirrors as a tool of observation.

Certainly, Felix Hartlaub used the mirror for self observational purposes, too, although they come to the fore mainly in his letters. For instance, on 15th January 1941 he writes to his father and stepmother:

My personal state is unfortunately but quite definitely below zero. Not sure whether this is still the aftermath of a bout of flu or whatever else. Every day is exactly the same sadness and inability to come to decisions by which I feel submerged, which can lead to an actual paralysis of my ability to think and speak. My face has lost any trace of intellectual imprint and is of a dullness that makes mirrors go blind.

Among his other main correspondents were his friends Irene Lessing, whose brother was to be the future husband of the writer Doris Lessing, and the man Irene would go on to marry, Klaus Gysi, a born survivor who formed part of the Communist resistance against Fascism and later became an influential figure in the cultural policy of the German Democratic Republic. Incidentally, Felix Hartlaub's great love in his short life was Klaus's sister, Erna Gysi, a Communist intellectual and friend of Alfred Döblin, who emigrated to France in 1938 but was later interned by the Vichy regime in Gurs (southern France).

This is not a who's who of the members of Germany's so-called "inner emigration", with whom Felix Hartlaub was directly or indirectly in contact, not to mention the circle of scholars and intellectuals in Heidelberg that influenced him, from the philosopher Karl Jaspers to the eminent legal scholar Gustav Radbruch. The young Hartlaub found himself in a situation in which he had to navigate with increasing care a web of suspicion, prejudice, slander and betrayal, eventually in close vicinity to the highest rank of Nazi officials in Hitler's entourage but with friends who were, in their majority, dedicated Communists. If ever there was a young eyewitness to the madness of his time, it was Felix Hartlaub, whose fragmentary oeuvre shows he had the potential to become a great writer, had he only survived the inferno of the final days of the war in Berlin.

II

Clouds over Paris is Hartlaub's diaristic chronicle of Paris over the course of a few months in 1941, roughly from the beginning of March until the end of August. The diary, a curious combination of matter-of-fact accounts and impressionistic narratives, novelistic snapshots and stylistically daring depictions of Paris, has as its backdrop the "absolute silence" to which the Parisians seemed to have condemned themselves, as Hartlaub put it in the aforementioned letter to his father dated 15th January 1941.

This literary impressionist begins his diary with a stunning depiction of the sky over Paris:

> The large patch of sky between the towers [of Saint-Sulpice]: bright, wet, juicy clouds en route north-east, proper clouds mostly, pot-bellied, with guts and heart, the odd simple scarf or banner among them. With necks bent, smoking brows, their chests, manes thrown forward. The sky between flushed a deep, fresh, purply-blue; inconceivably high, as if in another sky, thin cirrus starts to be spun, crossways to the cloud-drift. The west front, its back to the sun, deep black, blacker than soot, a wet, fragrant black. In certain places – column shafts, ledges – wind and

water have scrubbed, etched something, and white, pale bone-white, has seeped out.

This passage should be included in any anthology of literary depictions of cloud formations. To a certain extent, the composition of this literary canvas is emblematic of what is to come, as his impressions of the city betray the draughtsman in Hartlaub, whose original diary contains numerous sketches of Parisian scenes (reproduced on p. 159).

This diarist would like to belong to the Parisians but he senses, unsurprisingly given the oppressive circumstances, that he is met with suspicion; he keeps overhearing hostile comments ("C'est abominable – ces Boches... ils savent tout, – ils ne savent rien, et ils savent pourtant tout"). The embarrassing pretence of the occupier is precisely what Hartlaub wishes to distance himself from.

Critics have remarked that Hartlaub's diary suffers from a "complete lack of *I* and an absence of the warmth of life" (Katherine Roseau). This is undoubtedly correct, but one needs to add that this quality, what we could call the depersonalization of Hartlaub's diaristic narrative, is the result of his uneasiness with his situation as a German soldier in Paris. This also applies to the piecemeal perception that he offers in his diary: it is the direct equivalent to the fragmented existence that he leads as a German historian in the deserted Quai d'Orsay, fulfilling an utterly superfluous task, namely, examining all too well-known papers that offer insights into the past of fraudulent Franco-German relations.

Hartlaub suffers from the ambiguity with which he is perceived. His ideologically perverted fellow Germans see "something suspiciously Jewish" in his physiognomy, while the Parisians recognize in him, with his lack of elegance and clumsy accent, the inevitable German. Given these circumstances, our diarist resorts to what one might call "aesthetic minute-taking" as he provides a list of fragmented observations that link the strange, or rather offensive, symbols of the occupier with natural phenomena:

> The strands of rain slant down in confusion, buffeted by wind. The great swastika flag surges to the left, as if blown artificially with hot air, the pole flexing. [...] Suddenly, the sheeting rain lessens; glittering, wafting sparks as the sun bursts through, hot and stinging. Flashing slate on one side of the corner pavilion; to the left, in the park, dazzling fresh green. A great lake of acid blue, its edges soft, appears. The rain stops, as if someone had turned it off. The cobbles steam.

It is the urbanity of nature and the naturalness of the urbane that Hartlaub's diary celebrates when he abandons, momentarily, the surreal reality of German occupation. Incidentally, almost "naturally", it is the swastika flag that most often serves him for symbolic purposes. In this instance it stands for the self-inflated pretence of power; in the following sentence it foreshadows decline: "Half-eaten by the wind, the swastika flag on the top of the pediment flaps in constant ecstasy." (The original word Hartlaub uses, *knatternder*, has

another meaning: "crackling" or "rattling". It is tempting to
see in this acoustic image a variant of the famous final lines of
Friedrich Hölderlin's poem "Half of Life", given Hartlaub's
familiarity with this poet – in David Constantine's rendering:
"The walls stand / Speechless and cold, the wind / Clatters
the weathervanes.")

While the diary avoids the first person singular, it does
so in support of other voices – those of rustling leaves and
those of the German military personnel with their rattling
accents. There is something eerily atmospheric about the
way Hartlaub presents his observations and impressions.
Somewhat unusually for a young historian, he focuses on
the present and only occasionally connects his surround-
ings with their historical significance. We encounter the
familiar settings of the Faubourg Montmartre, the Place
Pigalle, even Fontainebleau, but only in passing. They do
not dominate the scene but provide the setting for particular
themes, often with ironic twists such as "Moonlight idyll in
Central Europe" at the time of the eleven-o'clock curfew
for Parisians. He perceives "dusky brutes", "blackouts" and
the "sequestered ministry", even an "international crisis at
the knocking-shop" (*Weltwende im Puff*). Hartlaub does so
with an alluring combination of sensory descriptions and
restrained sensuality, as if he wanted to play with his pro-
spective reader's imagination – definitely the hallmark of a
promising writer.

III

Nothing characterized Hartlaub's position in Paris better – both as a diarist and an historian – than the phrase "unhappy occupier" (Katherine Roseau). Through his fragmentary reflections, he attempted to overcome the discomfort with which he moved through his ideal city. However, the diary only reaffirmed his alienation from his official task. He knew that his sheer existence in Paris as an occupier was nothing but an imposition. His and his comrades' presence is a tall order for the city's inhabitants. And yet, he seemed to have sensed that keeping this diary was the most important education yet on his path to becoming a writer. His model in terms of descriptive precision was Paul Valéry's *Monsieur Teste*. But what he records is the "détresse" in Paris, the feeling of desolation, especially during the cold winter of 1940 with its shortage of coal and firewood. Hartlaub experiences "tristesse" and a sense of isolation, completely different from the life of the worldly Ernst Jünger, who found himself in better-heated hotels in the company of Cocteau, Céline, Guitry and Picasso, but also in the Musée de l'Homme where he meditated on ancient skulls and masks.

In one respect, though, they would have found common ground. The sense of despair and meaninglessness that became acute in the young Hartlaub is something that Jünger records from a letter he received from his mother at the time in which she observes, from the safe haven of the Alpine resort of Oberstorf, that the word "nothing" increasingly frustrates her in propagandistic phrases like "The people are everything – you yourself are nothing." Jünger comments: "The game of the nihilists becomes more and more transparent." Hartlaub, too, included a brief chapter on "propaganda" in his Paris diary, in light of the pathetic slogan that greeted Parisians in summer of 1941 on a large banner right across the Chambre des députés: "Germany wins on all fronts" – for Hartlaub a symbol of "pride comes before the fall", as indeed it did.

Hartlaub was in the process of becoming a writer who would have mastered the art of the interior monologue and sudden shifts of perspective, a virtuoso of imitating voices in writing, and an advocate of the "stream of consciousness" in literature. But, as his biographer Matthias Weichelt rightly argues in his perceptive study *The Absconded Witness*, Hartlaub was also a writer who, alongside his role model Franz Kafka, regarded literature as a space in which he could stand trial over himself. Hartlaub, this writer who ended up lost without a trace, displaced by fate, remains eminently identifiable through his diaries and letters as an invaluable voice from a time that was determined to extinguish all dissent. The "unhappy occupier" became a vanished chronicler and writer, from then on "occupied" himself by an enigma.

—RÜDIGER GÖRNER

SOURCES

Felix Hartlaub: *Kriegsaufzeichnungen aus Paris. Nachwort von Durs Grünbein. Mit Zeichnungen des Autors.* Suhrkamp Verlag, Berlin 2011.

Felix Hartlaub: *"In den eigenen Umriss gebannt". Kriegsaufzeichnungen, literarische Fragmente und Briefe aus den Jahren 1939 bis 1945.* 2 Vls. Ed. by Gabriele Lieselotte Ewenz. Suhrkamp Verlag, Frankfurt am Main 2007.

Katherine Roseau: "A Diary without the 'I': Embodiment and Self-construction in Felix Hartlaub's Extrospective Second World War Paris Writings" in *Textual Practice* 34 (2020), No 7, pp. 1123–1139.

Matthias Weichelt: *Der verschwundene Zeuge. Das kurze Leben des Felix Hartlaub.* Suhrkamp Verlag, Berlin 2020.

CLOUDS
OVER PARIS

MARCH 1941

Ventre de Paris, 1 March

The colonnades around the Bourse de Commerce, looking past towards the west front of Saint-Eustache. One
of the towers only got as far as the central pediment; the
other is also stunted, a scrawny stump, splinted with pillars.
The great gap between the two towers, the shallowness of
the pediment: a wide seat for a wide rump, the towers posts
for the arms to hang on to. Like Saint-Sulpice. The large
patch of sky between the towers: bright, wet, juicy clouds
en route north-east, proper clouds mostly, pot-bellied, with
guts and heart, the odd simple scarf or banner among them.
With necks bent, smoking brows, their crests, manes thrown
forward. The sky between flushed a deep, fresh, purply-blue;
inconceivably high, as if in another sky, thin cirrus begins
to be spun, crossways to the cloud-drift. The west front, its
back to the sun, deep black, blacker than soot, a wet, fragrant
black. In certain places – column shafts, ledges – wind and
water have scrubbed, etched something, and white, pale

21

bone-white, has seeped out. – The sun, as always on the Left Bank, sees only the side of the street facing it. Banished no more, as on frosty days, far beyond the crystal west – where, frozen to the sky, its light was no longer its own – the sun roves about, low, across the domes, in among the clouds. Sometimes it stays away altogether, and the buildings grow dim, nipped, for a brief moment, by cooler air.

The noise of the market then seems to grow, to spill out into the void, and the dazzling, bright house fronts turn yellow, compress, extend, buildings with six floors or more; French doors, more than one can number (trebled by all the open shutters, at some of which people appear), have sucked in the fading light. Is it about to rain? Then, stripped bare and washed clean, the light pulses back.

People queue outside a butcher's shop underneath the colonnade, pressed together along the wall. Beside them a somewhat remote policeman, to keep traffic flowing beneath the columns. No arms, his white truncheon poking out from under his cape the modest two centimetres or so prescribed, eyes (and ears) focused somewhere else entirely; some of the many queueing stare blankly at his back. The silence serves to amplify the echoing footsteps of passers-by and the yelping old-fashioned car horns; there is only the odd grumble from the queue. Their faces emptied, leached with waiting, defenceless in that stark, blinding light. Little eyes, whiskery women, brows unfurrowed, sweaty layers peeled off. The shadow of the columns falls across some of them. Their bodies apathetic beside each other. Apprentice girls with knitted brows, shaded by another's broad back, read cheap paperback novels, which they hold up close to their face. A black sign appears by the shop door, written in chalk: "Plus de tripes". A man, half-asphyxiated, his stomach pulled in, wriggles out past huge women, calling something over to a car. The sagging, empty, billowing shopping bags.

Tightly packed together, their noses pointing towards the Bourse, stand old-fashioned motors, beaten-up limousines now demoted to deliveries, basic little cars with trailers etc. The protruding rear sections, with boxes, trunks lashed on, stick well out over the pavement. Lorries drive past with huge, stripped animal carcasses swinging in disarray; stiff gestures from chopped-up limbs. Frozen meat, sewn into sackcloth. Great jolting carts – in the back of one that's empty stand two, three young men, in natty leather jackets, their hands on each other's shoulders. Legs criss-crossed for support, they bend their knees in unison over the bumps. The enormous horses, with swishing tails, and manes across their foreheads, sometimes fall into a little trot, the great empty cart barrelling along much too fast.

★

A passage leads straight into the transept of Saint-Eustache. It is eerily tall, narrow. A rudimentary rose window hangs overhead, of halting flamboyance, a great empty plate in the wall. Modern entrance, lots of statues in the ——, masked by a coagulated black film, like old cast iron. Looking up at the black branches of the double flying buttresses, right and left: pigeons, pigeon muck, weather-worn, shapeless gargouilles and finials. The same treatment on the outside of the apse as for the side aisles: fearfully thin pilasters, great shallow dos d'âne windows full of lacklustre tracery. A long way from the classical façade attached to the front; one can see the scar of the missing towers, a few smooth, bright ashlars against the sky.

The tops of bleached flat caps and berets form a level plane. A dozen policemen stand in front of the entrance to the transept, dotted along the pavement, some with red edges to their caps (Garde mobile?). Bent backs and grey beards among them. They each have their little number stitched in gold to their chest. Lots of waiting groups. Les Halles itself is closed; rubbish is being sluiced out with a hose. Worn leather jackets. Odd apprentice girls, in close-fitting white smocks and long boots, hands in pockets, among the men, smoking, scuffing their feet against the cool, dark cobbles. There are great panniers everywhere, oval in shape, with heads of lettuce, ranged up along the walls inside so that the central section remains clear. – Tired, dark lettuce leaves squashed between the thin wooden slats. A sudden smell of bay. A collapsing pyramid of oranges, wrapped in matt paper. Two nuns drag a heavy sack between them, streaking the floor. Their uncomfortable, dusty habits. The younger of the two, her head tipped back, wears a forced, apologetic smile. She has red cheeks and black, horn-rimmed spectacles. From her hunched companion there is only panting. – Out of a little wreck of a car, robbed of any insignia, there emerges a hulking great German soldier in a marine's uniform, his belt buckled in the final hole: a proper mess sergeant. He waves a friendly hello to one of the traders, standing there with legs splayed, slapping him on his leather shoulder. Then he lugs the heavy crate set aside for him to the car, his neck blood red.

Opposite the church the restaurant "Au nègre joyeux". Narrow frontages, the roofs varying hugely in height. One group of houses painted oxblood red. The cafés further along etc. almost empty; a few tables still with customers.

Rising water

The bridges are up to their shoulders in water. At the Pont Royal, with its wedge-shaped cutwaters, there is only half a metre to go before it reaches the high-water mark of seventeen whatever. Surging water, deep swirling holes behind the piers. The river has already engulfed the cast iron of the Pont de Solférino: chaos. The steps from the quais lead down into green water. The soft white porous stone of the embankment wall, stained yellow, blue, and that thick, green water. The trunks of the poplars, blacker than black – a living, breathing colour – stick out at an angle, the banks in which they are rooted submerged under metres of water. The plane trees have yet to get their feet wet, up on the street. Their bark like thick limewash. Where they have grown big and unchecked, the sky is dotted with their delicate, round seed pods. Opposite Notre-Dame. Tongues of ivy drape down over the embankment wall into the water. – An empty little barrel tries to go past on the floodwaters, leaping up, revolving on its axis.

The anglers propped up against the parapet, in position for hours on end, without swapping legs. The shorter ones among them have stones or boxes pushed underneath. Hanging off the bridges, on almost every one of the steps. So as not to intrude on somebody else's pitch, any of them. The noise of the water compared to the silence of all the people. The muting siege of the river. The stone of the thick wall is certainly warm today. – Some of the anglers have their wives with them, their interest more in the street, twisting their ankles. They're expected to get the catch straight in the pan. "Assez de matière grasse?" Quiet eddies behind the tree trunks and promontories along the embankment wall. One can imagine all the fish stopping there against the current, waggling their fins. The anglers mostly concentrate on these spots. With untold patience, the float(?) is constantly drawn down into the hiddenmost undercurrents, until [breaks off]

Tout seul, or: Le civil équivoque

Métro: the final two metres before the portillon automatique, where the ticket inspector sits. Your hand slips "inconspicuously" inside your coat – culs-de-sac in your handkerchief – to find your German city pass, light blue with darker stripes, in its cover of rippled Muscovy glass. Thin strips of leather around the edges, which flake off. You whip it out quickly, so that the inspector can only see a corner, and the people in front and behind you as little as possible. Or, with contrived pauses, you glance at it askance yourself, being careful not to show it to the inspector upside down. Strange contorted hand gestures. As if to say, "What, this? Just a German civilian pass. Thousands of them around. Nothing special." – The inspector sits there, his head level with the chests of people going by. One politely says "merci bien", another nods absent-mindedly, yet another offers no reaction whatsoever, simply puckering his lips, rooting around at something a little deeper in his mind, a flared nostril, the eyelids less heavy, a spark in the eyes, or they cloud over. Female inspectors: their faces ebb slightly, an imperceptible tightening, a trace of dilation in the pupils before they drift to one side. Others have seen, too, of course. You feel their eyes boring into your shoulders: pathetic shoulders in a loose spring coat (*impeccable, parisien*), the hunched, circumspect, sympathy-seeking back which would rather not exist. – Back and forth on the platform; you avoid walking past the inspector again. Hands in those vast, bottomless coat pockets: small change, bits of matchstick, paperclips, worn cinema tickets. The posters on the curved, tiled, whitewashed wall: fire insurance, opera performances, the newspaper Au Pilori, Secours d'hiver, the Berlitz School. Past the backs of fellow German soldiers to whom you feel no connection whatsoever. An expert eye takes in the epaulettes.

In the Métro carriage. Alone in the middle, he clasps the brass pole with both hands or hooks an arm around it. Isolement streams from every pore. A look down at the rest of the cargo, a wistful, amiable glance at the tops of children's heads. Attempts to smile at squaddies' conversations from a respectful distance. Time to get off, but squaddies are blocking the door: should he say "excuse me" in French or German? That hollow little moment of terror when he opens his mouth and says "Kamerad" or "Du": equable, close-lipped military German. So noisy: the adolescents around him, of both sexes, paying him no attention. His paletot gets caught in the doors as they snap shut; with his back towards the outside as it sails by, he stands in embarrassment en face of the other passengers. Casually crossing his legs and putting his hands in his pockets cannot alter the fact that he is held fast. Some are getting jumpy that he's blocking the door on purpose. "Je… descends moi-même," he stammers and at the next station is the first to leave the carriage, backwards. – Defunct, extinct Métro stations tear past outside. Naturally, there is another ticket inspector here, too, with a large leather bag and a soft conductor's cap, squashed down over his eyes. Raising his head and fixing his little black eyes on him – another lesson learnt – he silently notes the flash of blue in his breast pocket. The temperature around him drops. Deflated arguments, suddenly baseless, drag on… Desolation grows…

But he knows the Métro better than the natives. Havre–Caumartin, onze heures. Someone's lost: standing perplexed in the sparkling, empty tunnel with its glazed tiles; the last trains drone on through. A big man, a bit drunk, his head muzzy with red wine, the odd grey hair, a slight squint in one eye: "Pardon, monsieur, à l'Odéon, quelle direction est-ce?" The other man, tapping his nose with his finger, launches into a short lecture, illustrated by means of the illuminated panel. "Vous n'êtes pas français?" "…" "Alors, monsieur, vous êtes allemand, et moi, je suis français…, et moi, j'habite depuis quinze ans vis à vis de l'Odéon… et vous, vous voulez m'expliquer, comment y aller…" Another lecture. The Frenchman, his eyes reeling, pulling a face in disgust, must concede that the other chap actually does know his stuff, and has named the only remaining connection. He retreats across the platform in a desperate slant: "C'est abominable – ces Boches… ils savent tout, – ils ne savent rien, et ils savent pourtant tout."

Place Pigalle

Evening: total blackout, a deep, dense sky, with a warm breeze. Serried groups of soldiers and girls coming towards him. He dodges out of the way, stepping into the street. The steep cobbled streets leading up the hill echo to the sound of hobnail boots, irregular, intermittent; at the bottom there are a few faint, faded banners reading "Hotel". Further up, solid blackness. A number of soldiers around one girl, who directs the stumbling circle about her. The girls seem curiously small to him, young. The purposefulness of those scuttling stiletto heels, the stumbling, scuffing, sparking of the hobnail boots. One after another the groups drift by, easily broken up by anything obstructing the flow: a huge great sergeant submits, with a slurring bass voice, to the please, please, come, come, come from two cajoling girls. Another, his ample coat tugged at by various people with the addresses of various hotels: "Gerrof, will ya… I've already ha' a skinful"… The surging plane trees along the centre of the Boulevard de Clichy. Suspicious groups of adolescents, smoking, their hats pushed back, emerge from the public conveniences, of which there are an abundant number. Tripping over heaps of earth, barriers both with lights and without. The silent patrol of midnight-blue "flics". They conduct low, improbably polite conversations. You only realize they're there once you're right on top of them. Between the tree trunks an inextricable, motionless form: a soldier, huge in his greatcoat, and a girl, hair and a couple of handfuls of scrawny back, wrapped around each other and lost to the world. At the edges of the pavement, where a bluish half-light constantly swashes out of the swing doors, clusters of adolescents – tiny faces weighed down by voluminous quiffs, sideburns, spots, long hair down the backs of their necks, in half-open trench coats, with loosely tied neckerchiefs. Motionless, they watch the mêlée wide-eyed as it stumbles and drifts, breaks up. If a girl is pushed aside, dropped for a moment, they try to sidle up to her, with a half-patronizing, half-despondent "Alors, la petite, on va monter ensemble?"… They earn a shrug at best – in this part of the city the German army reigns en maître absolu. Over by the doorways on the other side of the "stream", their shoulders bathed in a faint blue glow, absorbing what little light there is, lurk the krakens of the cove. Get any closer and you'll encounter battleaxes with night-piercing, eagle-like stares and pitted, crudely painted faces. – When the main flow breaks up, the two groups are left facing each other, with no connection whatsoever. – Nearly all the successful encounters are consummated in the deepest darkness – with unerring sense, the soldiers, more or less all of them drunk, entirely incapable of speech, find what they want: the non-professionals, quite young, the modistes, couturières who have flocked here from all over the city or recently relocated. – C'est au moins ce qu'ils disent – qui n'ont plus de travail. "C'pas mon métier – mais pour ne pas crever de faim…"

The countless little cafés, one after the other, seem to have boosted their numbers, their doors in constant motion; groups of squaddies, pushing their heads through the blackout portière, stomp in, go round once in the revolving door, then outside again, dazed: "God, there's not much going on here…" He lets himself be swept along by one such charge, then stays inside on his own by the counter. A kind of quiet – the roar is outside – a shimmering desert of empty little tables, multiplied by the mirrored walls. Perhaps a violinist at the back, inviting movement from his knees, his hips… Along the bar, adolescents and pimps, with contrived nonchalance, and without altering position, all try to catch his eye. He joins them, orders a drink in a halting, croaky voice, his French deliberately incorrect, pays straight away, even though no one has asked him to, rounding up generously. Wearing a leather or blue cotton apron, his sleeves rolled up, the barman, with various washed-out facial features, a deformed, unbalanced head, le surveille du coin de l'œil. He himself tries not to look anywhere in particular, only to be confronted by his reflection in every direction… the tormented furrowed brow, the sweaty nose, the little, drooping, lipless mouth. Nevertheless, he tells himself that, altogether, he exudes a kind of danger, repulsion, at the same time as being almost invisible, apologetically nullifying his own shape. A squaddie with a blustering red face comes in, trying to peer through the shimmering void. He addresses him coyly, swapping elbows on the zinc bar: "Fancy a beer?"… The squaddie rolls his eyes, puts on a quarter-smile, but stands mulishly silent in the doorway. He's so completely and utterly plastered – pretty much impossibly so – that this dark-haired man-cub can risk asking him in fluent German; he's past caring tonight. He doesn't get any further with the beer: a raucous reveller suddenly reappears, and the squaddie is off, swallowed up by the night. The lines deepen on the furrowed brow of the consommateur – a pained feel to the place; it even startles two sailors, right au fond, in a kind of séparé, with their arms wrapped around a girl, each murmuring ineffable little songs.

By mischance, he manages to end up in one café twice on the trot. One time he succeeds in getting into conversation with a young soldier, asserting several times that he used to be a one himself; he almost pulls out his service book. The young rifleman is rather gloomy: "Every woman here is for the taking. Bitches, the lot of 'em. Whatever their age. There was one over there, in a posh fur coat. No chance. Then a purser walks past, gives her the eye; up she gets and they're off. German women are different. More modest. More hygienic, too. But you have to admit: it's all go here. We've had a high old time of it. Broken our promises(?), too. We've pissed all over them old v——s, though, I can tell you. They never notice a thing in the dark. There was one there, filthy bitch, she'd catch your five-mark piece in her v——. But me and my mate, we heated one up with a lighter. That gave her something to squawk about. Strasbourg–Saint-Denis, first right, round the corner: you can watch all thirty-two positions. Two women, with a rubber thing, this long and so thick, poking it into each other. I couldn't shake it for days. And they had this electrostatic gadget thing which they ran all over their bodies. Whooping away, they were. But they were so old and fat..."

★

Outside, he surrenders to the adolescents: with a magnanimous "alors" which soon clears the field; he calls out to two girls as their silhouettes sail past, but gets nowhere. He hardly receives a reply. The pair forge ahead into the path of two approaching soldiers... He walks alongside, but is forced back by lamp posts, couples rooted to the spot, loses his quarry in the dark, and cannot find them again.

"Alors, mademoiselle, qu'en pensez-vous...?"

"..."

"Vous êtes pensive… méchante…"

"…"

"Vous n'avez pas le temps pour faire un peu…"

"Faire quoi?"

"… faire l'amour… Que pensez-vous?"

"…"

"Si vous voulez boire quelque chose… on pourrait entrer là."

They look each other in the eye in the harsh light, with [blank] eyelids. She sees he is almost translucent with exhaustion, his eyes pricked with tears. "Mais vous n'êtes pas allemand, voyons…" "Mais si… oui, je le suis, et j'ai été soldat, mais on m'a réclamé…" etc. etc. "Vous savez, je n'aime pas les civils." The girl has a round, stumpy head with a low, rather mean brow and a great scar of a mouth. Her friend makes an effort for them to escape.

★

"Vous êtes seul?" asks the waitress once he has picked his way through the packed restaurant to the last empty table. She spreads out a paper tablecloth, clinking cutlery, bread, salt. He cranes his neck, runs his fingers round his collar. "Est-ce que vous cherchez quelque chose?" "Pas… rien…" From now on, he only looks at his plate, like a child at its own little table. Whenever a new course arrives, he whispers a flat "merci bien". On occasion, he furtively wipes the sweat from his brow, from around his neck. His waistcoat is tight: he has acquired such a belly. A fashionable, if slightly uncomfortable red leather sofa, the table too far away. He is sitting in a séparé of sorts, by a mirrored wall. The back of the sofa, which stands obliquely to the mirror, forms a side wall. Across the back, a planter with artificial azaleas in artificial sea-green moss. He leans his right shoulder against his reflection in the mirror; opposite is another glass wall in which he appears again:

The forlorn face. Well-fed, but glum and ill-shaven. He tries to fashion a chin, fingering his improbably flabby cheeks. A young French workman in engine-fitter's overalls at the comptoir: his taut, slightly concave cheeks, the metallic sheen across the cheekbones, the bronze skin, like tanned leather. – He touches the ice-cold tip of his nose. His face is flushed by a demi-carafe de Beaujolais, tears well up in his eyes, the mirror seems to darken. The noise of the restaurant is more harmonious, whether from far away or close to. He leans against the mirror, and turns his head away, seeing only the blurred reflection of his nose in the corner of his eye.

One time he is together with a "colleague", a PhD: blond sideburns, dissipated forehead, dry, thin, raked-back hair, dry, translucent skin. They sit beside each other on the ostentatious banquette, the backs of their heads glued to their mirror image. They speak little, in fits and starts, slobbering their soup. The philosopher acts as if he were a cross between Diogenes and Pyrrho, and wears a silk shirt and bow tie. His mouth frozen like a scar from a lightning strike. Curt, awkward gestures. "W-w-w-well?" He has no bottom. The hem of his jacket, which hangs straight down, is a wavy line. Muscular shoulders, a sinewy hand. – Copious amounts of wine make him relax for a few minutes, the veins protruding on his forehead. "He" turns round in his seat, immersing himself in his reflection. Departing Frenchmen remark: "Faux ménage." – –

The icy ring of alienation and mistrust he has cast about him. He is firmly pinned down within it, his gestures winning no space, his words lacking the air to carry. He is much more restricted talking to Germans, with their specific physical features. A crew cut, pince-nez and a fat neck are much more readily accepted; their appearance only puts a stop to the conversation for a second or two. Whereas for him, that moment of horror stretches out into a small eternity: drawn cheeks, the nostrils stiff, mouths turned to stone. He does everything he can to ease and expedite identification: quickly unfolding a German newspaper, bringing out a Baedeker. He intentionally speaks poor French, orders beer, cold, thin, interminable. Once, absorbed by a French book, he forgot.

Three men sit down at the next table... "Face de la collaboration... les salauds... les pillards... ce n'est pas encore fini" etc. He squirms, clears his throat, looks away, cranes his neck to find the garçon. Only when he is paying do the others notice him, his soldier's ration card. He saves himself by knocking over his chair, and thinks he hears: "Manque d'éducation, de tact... espèce de fou assez dangereux..." etc.

A couple in the neighbouring séparé, back-to-back with him. Muffled words into each other's shoulders, the silence of long kisses. The couple leave, eyeing him as they go past, in his empty red mirrored compartment. He returns their gaze: benign, full of admiration, and at the same time veiled, not quite there.

In a student café on the Boulevard Saint-Michel. He had been there once before, five, eight years ago, with the Fellowship for Reconciliation. The waiter calls the students "tu"; one of them gets given some money. Little round tables, a hard horsehair sofa. Right next to him are two young students, in coats, belts dangling down, collars turned up; one has a thin moustache, both with long, combed-back hair. They fix their dark, almost childlike eyes on him, unblinking; arched eyebrows. Before them lies a map showing the theatre of war in North Africa. An older student is about to sit down with them, follows their gaze, then stays where she is. Lots of little lines around the eyes, across the forehead, with too much make-up carelessly applied; one strand of hair has gone grey. He pays immediately the consommation arrives, elaborately, with high-denomination Occupation Reichmarks – the coffee is *"national"** and scalding hot – turning his bag inside out in search of something to read, to give his eyes something to do. Suddenly gets up, without having had breakfast, almost upsetting the tray in the process, with numerous croaky *"pardon"*s. He gives the girl an all-encompassing look: sorry... [Blank]

By the door, he thinks he hears her say: "Celui-ci n'était pas si mal." Was he mistaken?

---

*   *Café national* was the term used during the war for coffee made from other ingredients, such as acorns or chickpeas.

APRIL 1941

Quartier latin

Rising up from the east – which has been a wall of purple the whole afternoon – a heavy bank of cloud lies stretched across the rooftops. From the west, a harsh light the colour of brass. It just touches the garrets, chimneys, the uppermost storey on one side of the street, with a luminous, furnace-like heat. From the opposite direction there are short, half-choked gusts of cold wind. A pigeon is held, suspended, above the rooftops on air rising up from the narrow street below. It did rain for a moment, the cobbles peppered black, but now only a few parched drops fall from the sky. The heat of summer, bleakly odourless, already covers the streets. A rain-black evening sharpens one's hearing – but the searing light up on the rooftops, at the windows, deadens the ear. In the depths of the street purple and grey prevail. The surface of the house fronts protrudes, recedes, imperceptibly. Myriads of tall windows contract to slits the width of a line. Most of them with no volets, just bare incisions without any real horizontals to speak of, and yet these houses, as they retreat, seem infinitely alive, familiar, almost human. The many shades of grey, yellow. The occasional little banner, "Hôtel", slightly bent, loops down a building. Greengrocers' shops, two metres wide, still open, a couple of bunches of radishes, carrots, left. Tired tulips piled up on top of each other, all the stalks pointing the same way. Books and antiques on display in every other window. Bareheaded despite the threat of rain, "he" has not yet had supper, devouring the shop windows. In one – often they are several rooms deep – a solitary electric light bulb burns on an enormous chandelier dripping with crystal. The proprietor – hunched back, dark suit, grey hair, elegant – in conversation with an elderly couple, falls silent as "his" shadow fixes itself to the outside window. The pavement is so narrow, he is unable to step back to determine the name. On the other side, even more "Antiquités"… he plants himself across the street, before crossing back again, then on up the street in a highly suspicious zigzag – who in this day and age has that much time on their hands, and such fat cheeks? – the street is never-ending. He sees all the chairs – his cheeks mirroring the upholstery – floating on tapering, fluted Empire-style legs, or swaying on the springy, muscular legs of the rococo, with splayed claws. Bluish-pink, pale-green silk damask covers. Engravings, lithographs, of the dix-huitième. The legs of the couple intertwined with those of the chairs: tiny feet, the slow, even swell of a leg – the knees still a way away, shy, concealed humps in the choppy expanses of skirt; his tight silk socks, faultlessly sculptured trousers…

The bergères, divans

They can't be comfortable: they've got that same gilt carved wood everywhere. Chunky, solid little books. He reads the spines… La nuit et le moment – Le Sopha – Mémoires secrètes – Mémoires du comte de Stern Stern Stern. One shop window unfurnished save for some heavy fabric, concertinaed together. He wished he could name them: brocade, satin, soie brochée – what does broché mean? – what's petit point? The soles of his feet hurt; he would rather like to adjust his belt (his stomach's rumbling); he can see the reflection of his Adam's apple going up and down in the window. He'd like to look at two, three knick-knacks at once; if only he had the eyes of a chameleon. The next shop, and the lateness of the hour, pulls him on. Considering things: holding, stroking, pressing them to your stomach, holding them between your legs. – A Buddha's head made out of a very hard, grey-green stone – granite, syenite? – with a protruding chin. Noh masks with real hair and chubby, smiling cheeks with blushing red circles on them. Or a worm-eaten wooden sculpture from the late Middle Ages, heavily painted: reddish gold, carmine red, dark green. An angel, both arms missing, with bulging cheeks; a pietà. – But there is no way he could go in, even though the shops are largely still open.

He comes out, via the Rue de l'Université, onto the square by Saint-Germain-des-Prés – here the light can reach further down. The chestnut trees – their leaves already the length of your finger, but not yet forming a complete canopy – stand beside each other, breathless, in lines of golden green. The various bits of masonry arrayed in the square – finials, propped-up gargoyles, the rustic brown stone of the tower – baking in a reddish light.

The ostinato of pigeons cooing somewhere between the leaves and the wall, and the swish and squawk of caged birds in a window.

Rue de Seine. He meets a "colleague". The one who wrote that important book on the idea of the state in the late Middle Ages. He appears to be slightly drunk. Grey Tyrolean hat with a middling brim, thick octagonal glasses, no neck, a reddened face – trench coat with a twisted belt, epaulettes. "Am I pleased to see you... I just came across something over there, Rue Bonaparte, I think it was... these great plates, wrought copper, or they could be brass – for my hall – I still have the estate. But the price was scandalous... Come down here, should be just on the left. You know this, I presume, the house where Racine died, in the Rue Visconti. Quite big. Look, there's another plaque... Adam Mienciewicz*... do you know who he was? Oh no? Polack chap. It's amazing how steeped in history everything is. Quite wonderful. Ooh, look at those sconces. They would work in the hall, too. What are they called in French? I'll just pop in..."

At the end of the Rue de Seine, the dome of the institute still in [breaks off]

---

* i.e. Adam Mickiewicz (1798–1855), the great Polish poet.

Evening stroll...

The Panthéon, seen from the Île Saint-Louis, through the wide gap of the rue Jean-du-Bellay. A huge sky, into which a mass of houses and rooftops – the ragged ridges, teeming chimneys, crags of slate – occasionally protrude; superimposed on top is the infinite expanse of the Panthéon with its straight roof, creating an even skyline over which only the dome is permitted to assert itself, inflated with gentle, measured breaths. Into a tall sky made up of large, identical bits of cloud. Only the odd exposed patch where gold and dark blue emerge. It seems to be blowing hard up there. A fine even haze. Sans éclat, the sun has been soaked up by the fine, matt, powdery twilight. To the left, just down the hill, Saint-Étienne-du-Mont seems to be a little less secure on that sea of rooftops than the Panthéon. The houses wash up against the church, which lists slightly. The tower with its pierced lantern, just on the one side; fears for the attached west front, thin as fretwork when viewed side-on. But that elongated pontoon of a slate roof, as if made from sheet iron, with neither seams nor hatches: unsinkable, incombustible. Beyond emerges the broader, horned tower of Sainte-Geneviève(?), tucked into the Lycée Henri-IV. Huddled against the transept façade of Saint-Étienne is the tower stump of the École Polytechnique, as yet unaffected by the elements in a new yellow-green imperméable. – The timeless class of the grey and blue in which the buildings are clad; their pores seem to exude it, imperceptibly, like smoke.

The reflection of the Seine carries the pale brightness of the western sky away to the left, to the east. Approaching frost spices the air, yet the weeping willow which leans out over the river from the Square Notre-Dame is already covered with green. The thick, broad crowns of the chestnut trees, which, neither discoloured nor deformed, have managed to retain all that frost and moisture and hold up the snowy sky, are now seized with white foam, pale bursting stars.

The houses along the Quai de Béthune...

Broad, simple surfaces, one flowing smoothly into the next, taking the course set before modifying it slightly, imperceptibly following the curve of the river. It is difficult for the light to break away; they hold it back. All of them are painted in the same milky white, but each with a different gentle shade in tone: pink, olive green, yellow ochre. No balconies, narrow ledges, decorative trim. Everywhere that elegant design of large, flat windows: hundreds of them, trebled in number by the open shutters and subdivided by the simple knee-high grilles. One never tires of seeing them. The shutters – evenly distributed, genteelly purblind – present a harmonious group of short dashes. There is an austere garland motif, only just visible due to the thick coat of paint, over the windows of one of the houses, repeated countless times and yet not hackneyed. Another is divided up by thin, slender pilasters.

They are all very tall, several storeys taller than the mighty old poplars along the embankment. One can count another six, seven garrets in addition, often in two rows. Some are a bit lower than others, the steep front face of the slate roof, from which the dormer windows stick out, coming further down. Simple, wide entranceways, with a faun's mask at the keystone, or supported by two slightly protruding caryatids. The windows of older narrow frontages with no shutters, only a bare wall with vertically incised rectangles – but the effect is not bleak: the surface curves imperceptibly outwards or gently in, drawing in its coat of whitewash or shedding it in flakes. – One house front near the bridge, every crack blinded with white – blue and purple seem to flow beneath, the window frames, the meagre decoration made of soft grey-green limestone. Travertine? One can read the words Institut polonais, Bibliothèque Mienkiewicz... Past the Pont Sully to the Hôtel Lambert, which belongs to the Czartioriskys.* Its walls, encased in the heavy armour of rustic work, curve around the tip of the island. The large arched windows are piled up with sandbags, right to the top. – As the daylight on them dies away, they begin to glow of themselves, the dry, grainy white turning to glistening mother-of-pearl, a blossoming pink...

The anglers, strangely short-necked with all the windows staring down at their backs, compressed under the height of the buildings. Somewhere the shutters swing closed, with a

---

* i.e. Czartoryski. The exiled Polish statesman Adam Jerzy Czartoryski (1770–1861) lived at the Hôtel Lambert from 1843 onwards.

gentle sigh. A female figure, bare arms against the window grille, from under a shawl. On one of the floors a window closes, smoothly, without any force; a slight tremble of glass. Lazy smoke floats up from a barge.

BAUDELAIRE A MIEUX DIT.

Quai…

The thick white wall of the quai. Soft stone with large pores. North side of the Île Notre-Dame, in shade. Abandoned painters' easels leaning against the wall. The Seine has fallen hugely, the bridge opposite with its empty niches above the cutwaters looks almost like it is on stilts. By the embankment wall, the section of the collapsed bridge which linked the two islands is in the throes of being knocked off. Groynes in the middle of the river, surrounded by wooden scaffolding, receiving attention. A shallow boat with a red sail sits motionless in the current. The opaque brown-green of the water. The anglers hold their rods vertically down the embankment wall, the water dropping away from them. One can already feel the full thirst of summer. The towers of the Conciergerie pressed close one behind the other, a dull gleam from its cones of slate. Dazzling, towering clouds above. The Hôtel-Dieu, a thousand blue lunettes, their haunches wet, cold and black. Waves of cold air through the gateways, up

from the river. Across on the sunny side of the embankment
there are people sitting in the sun, opposite Saint-Gervais.
Only the steep slate roof, straight and unbroken, and the
gable end of the transept rise up over the cluster of tall, thin
houses along the embankment. The roof sits high up on
the back of the baroque façade affixed to the west front. It
drops away steeply over the chancel, only at the last moment
revealing [breaks off]

The houses are largely only two to three windows wide,
their frontages in a single plane, moving in consort: belly,
hips, funnel chest. The roof has difficulty in deciding whether
to abandon the vertical, extending into garrets, bulky chimneys, requiring one, two bends to make it to the ridge. Eaves
of varying height. The finish: all different kinds of white,
ochre, pale green. The shutters, their slats stuffed with paper,
another white yet again. The washed out, rough-hewn stone
with which the chimneys are edged. All this brightness, in
the searing light of a stormy afternoon, against that blue
slate which cuts short the pale blue of a spring sky, suffused
with fine gleaming dust. Above the roof there is the broad,
squat, unassuming tower, two windows next to each other,
the view from each of which is directed towards the ground
by louvres with three slats. The whole building sparkling,
dazzling, and yet in many ways muffled, shrouded in smoke
pricked with golden dust; one cannot tell if the air is warm
or cold. Smoke from scorched stone. And the damp of the
riverbed.

The colours at street level – shops, awnings – cut in half
by the embankment wall. The dull yellow trunks of the

plane trees, their branches covered in the first signs of spring, submerging into the coloured façade.

Across the river to the north-west, the Tour Saint-Jacques, curiously isolated, like a relic, above the long, tall block of houses on the Quai de la Mégisserie. The corner pillars put one in mind of a withered, woody ornamental thistle; the silvery colour, too. Or one thinks of a weathered, hewn chunk of coral. Crowned on the one side by the great statue of the saint. – The tall houses, girt with common, narrow balconies (on the last floor but one), beneath a common, curved zinc(?) roof, out of which up to three rows of dormer windows have been claimed, in the unobtrusively elegant gold-grey brown of the nineteenth century. The sky draws damp and mist; towering clouds beyond, of which one can only see the caps and crests, their bodies and feet lost in the haze.

In an open window, a well-groomed man with silver hair, in a brown velvet jacket and a panama hat, looks across at the opposing bank, which is inflamed in a white, dusty light. One can feel the cold which still dominates the apartments.

Autre promenade

Rue Tournon towards the Luxembourg Gardens. Rain: take cover. The walls of the buildings the deepest of blacks, setting off the first raindrops which fall slowly, at a strange angle. Behind, above the Gardens, the depths of a restless, glaring world of gathering clouds. Monstrous towers, the yellow of sulphur, pile up in a somewhat uneven sky of insipid blue, mixed with greeny-yellow. A number of these billowing fortresses one behind the other, their shadows purple, brown; more and more grow, rise up, before they are driven under, buried by a low, coursing, shapeless blanket; and with it, the rain.

The lower central pavilion, with a shallow dome over the gateway. The larger, hulking great pavilions in the corners. Stone studded with stone, bolted, the pillars stricken with bands of rustic work which in places have washed white. The strands of rain slant down in confusion, buffeted by wind. The great swastika flag surges to the left, as if blown artificially with hot air, the pole flexing. The airman, in his greatcoat, with neither buttons nor belt, a sub-machine gun on a wide strap. He crosses over to the second of two sentry boxes painted with red, white and black stripes; the first is being cleaned by two French workmen in berets: a bucket of water is poured over, before they set to with scrubbing brushes. The rain plays its part. A lieutenant appears in the gateway, looks up at the rain cloud, hesitates. At a window in the right-hand corner pavilion, an NCO, seemingly with nothing on under his black drill jacket, yawns at the drumming rain.

Suddenly, the sheeting rain lessens; glittering, wafting sparks as the sun bursts through, hot and stinging. Flashing slate on one side of the corner pavilion; to the left, in the park, dazzling fresh green. A great lake of acid blue, its edges soft, appears. The rain stops, as if someone had turned it off. The cobbles steam.

Along the railings. The two bronze dancers, a scarf curling above them like a skipping rope, hurry into the gardens with glistening wet rumps. Box hedges, seized by the sun, spray thousands of sparks. The bushes already almost entirely covered with frizzy green.

The date and peanut sellers at the entrance to the park. Visitors to the gardens with chairs, children and perambulators still sheltering under the low roof of an erstwhile stall. Everywhere the white, yellow, pinkiness of burst chestnut buds – you need to hear it for yourself: the bursting, foaming, the ringing drips, and something like a thousand-voice [breaks off]

Porte Saint-Martin

The right-hand pavement climbs, the road dropping away to the left, steps leading down. Below, in the dip, the gateway, like a gravestone, seen side on. The arch bursting with entablature, brickwork rising up from below. – White, with purple shadows and delicate golden-brown, grey-green stains, strangely phosphorescent in the twilight. The trophy-topped pyramids, cut in relief, which flank the road beneath, protrude slightly, indecipherable. The fronts of old-fashioned houses, three times as tall as the arch, sullenly recede, faceless, a wasteland de noblesse, diluted through proliferation; even the windows are fossilized, like occult spavin, d'un air renfrogné. The sky quite blotted out, but still bright, even though the sun went down some time ago: a high, thin, greeny-blue. The gathering darkness seems unable to flow in, like on glossy paper. A cold wind blows down the boulevard. The moon, half-full, like a forgotten faint impression of itself which, minutes later, will have faded completely. Instead, it takes on a coppery skin, and begins, of itself, to glow. – Loose bands of squaddies, confident of their way without stopping, plenty of bare street between their legs. Disappearing into Métro stations, which are jolted awake by the sound of their boots; the noise becomes too much. German civilians among them; one, round-shouldered, with a drooping violet-reddish brown suit. He trails one step behind, spitting both ways before being the first to climb into a covered truck which has been loaded up with all kinds of beds and mattresses. One after the other, the soldiers climb sluggishly over the running board in the drop tailgate. Nothing to hold on to. – The blind man sitting with his legs stretched out across the pavement, his head leaning against the poster column, improvising on an accordion, seemingly in concert with the gusts of wind, beating time with his head. – Beyond, in the west, where the two walls running alongside the street finally converge, and the street drops away, the sky is still a pale yellow.

★

Easter Eve. The smoky, grey sky begins immediately the roofs leave off. When you look out, you get fine droplets on your nose and eyelids. The cobbles peppered with dark spots, gradually turning wet black, but no sheen. It is only as the houses start to turn murky that you realize dusk is setting in; the sky maintains its pale, lazy brightness.

Rue Aboukir etc. Time and again one discovers afresh the Place des Victoires with its equestrian king. Sometimes you look at the horse's croup and the blazing tail, out of which the whole thing grows, sometimes between the outstretched, nation-eclipsing forelegs, the tousle-haired, laurel-wreathed Louis above. A little arena of enrapture, chopped up by the incisions of wide streets. Traces of gold, bronze, brown on the concave faces of the buildings that remain. The sagging rooflines, the pilasters a little flat-chested under thick limewash, too many chimneys, garrets, attic storeys packed on top.

Suddenly, your gaze is drawn along the long wall of the central post office, stiff with columns, black with mould. – At the end of a wide, twilit street: a dark core to that thick, deadening air, a pavilion of the Louvre.

Rue Montmartre, Rue des Petits-Carreaux

It smells of fish, although almost all the shops are shut, the lorries gone. Cabbage and lettuce leaves on the ground. Dogs poke their noses underneath. Electric light in empty butchers' shops on bare, freshly washed marble slabs; some bay the only living thing. Butchers with bare arms, hands on hips. Retractable grilles are pushed across. There are still people in the bakers', the long loaves of bread tucked under their coats against the wet. Most of the shop fronts are covered up with panels of dull, red-brown or green sheet metal, with metal bars and ties. The electric light does not reach the street, illuminating only inside, like a fish tank. One café-bar after the next. The last consommateurs lean against the comptoir, [blank]

The woman at the till has left her perch, the garçon wiping the tables, sweeping up the sawdust. Intimate conversations, sotto voce, the *patron* or the cashier either right at the heart of it, or to one side, fiddling with something on the counter, watching passers-by outside. Or the sound of constant moaning, protracted stories – between all the leaning in, the pauses for breath – echoing around the empty room. – All those black plaques by the entranceways with gold writing. All that gold-black lettering on the buildings. A faun's head with furrowed cheeks [blank] Across the street: all the windows have those heads as corbels, pure Louis XV.

Buttes Chaumont

April. The wind burrows up through the lush green grass, already the depth of a hand. A narrow sandy path slanting away towards the slope leads up the first butte. Abandoned higgledy-piggledy cast-iron chairs. Strong sunshine and an east wind cross [blank]

Trees surge. The blossom on the chestnuts still brown, the leaves only half unfurled. Most of the plane trees are quite bare, bristling with old seed pods. Tiny sprouting leaves – frizzy, reddish-green – on the odd branch, like tendrils from another plant. The area is very exposed, defenceless against the north and east wind. Only the bushes in hollows are saturated with a pale, even green. The catkins, thousands of dangling yellow strokes, never quite at peace – constantly torn to one side, hoisted up to the clouds. Restless cloudscapes, drawing greyish-purple shadows, with luminous, smoking edges, across the city. At the foot of the northern slope, on the banks of the lake, wayward cedars flail about. A grammar-school boy sits above the green slope, right in the wind, reading a book on a flimsy chair, his mane of blond hair streaming. "Racine – Andromaque". The balustrades and steps are made of grey concrete, mimicking tree trunks, with knot-holes, bare patches with no bark etc.

On the second butte, bits of rock poke out which have been shored up with concrete. A muses' temple with nothing inside, a magnet for adolescents. Boys discuss a mate's girlfriend: "Et se montrer avec cela aux Buttes Chaumont…" The patter of children's feet on all the steps, on the terraces. A view vertically down onto the lake, its surface chequered by the intersecting waves. A plum tree leans out over it, with its little pink buds. A dark-headed duck with a shiny yellow beak.

FELIX HARTLAUB

Place des Vosges

The first proper spring evening, everything pure, in equilib-
rium. The sky way up high and at the same time close to;
it has drawn damp from every rooftop and yet is lit up by
nothing but purply-blue, an even gold. Every street lies in
shadow. From some distance, you can see the east side of
the square at the end of Rue des Francs-Bourgeois gleaming
in full sun: red and yellow-white, and the golden glimmer
of the simple, steep, slate roofs.

The square is still not quite used to the crisp, fresh green
of the chestnuts. It clashes with the red of the brick. The
leaves, although almost full-grown, keep close together, in
anticipation, intimation of blossom. The complete internal
structure of the tree, as demonstrated in winter, is still
there. The tree remains a flower head, a huge umbel. The
hornbeams at the edge of the square, cut back into a twiggy
hedge, are still almost bare. Incessant sparrow noise. A
number of them are taking a dust bath. Children, ten to
twelve years old, boys and girls, playing cops and robbers
between the shaped lawns, fountains, chairs. The princesses,
pushed and pulled this way and that, then released by the
robbers, show no sign of wanting to flee... "Ne fais pas la
brute"... "Au secours!" The west side of the square is still
streaked with light. The rusticated bases and window surrounds, the protruding keystones cast broad shadows, the
chimneys sending great swathes of shadow eastwards, over
the slate roofs. In the west, between two slate mansard

54

roofs which drop steeply down to meet each other, is the sun, broken in two by a chimney. Despite its pushing back the wall of light, it is impossible to look at due to the glare; the light's arrival in the sky is beyond the means of any eye. The roofs in front, in their own shadow, still look too cold, too precipitous for the light, the chimneys jutting out, haggard, into the sky. The red of the bricks stale, the ledges shrivelled, downcast.

The stockiness of the arcades. The columns, in their heavy, rusticated armour, seem half-sunk in the new cobble-stones.

Une impression

A cold east wind along the banks of the Seine, early morning. Dust mixed with fluffy, golden-brown plane-tree seeds which catch on the fresh horse droppings. The defunct Dépôt de Sauvetage, the two vast plane trees opposite the German employment agency. Their trunks are painted white-yellow-white in broad rings; those waiting gather there in the afternoons. No queue as yet, but people are arriving thick and fast, across from the Chambre des députés, head-on into the wind and dust, noses behind scarves, furs. Berets, worn winter coats. Drooping red eyelids. Two flics, très gentils, provide information – laboriously, tirelessly – issuing numbers, giving advice. One of the women takes

measures against the sand blown up by the biting wind. All
in black, a loose, threadbare coat, woollen shawl and mittens.
From underneath her insubstantial beret, grey with dust,
streams thick, jet-black hair; she shields her face and hair
with a shapeless mittened hand. Broad, sallow face, stale
face powder or pockmarks, large lips painted red below
the suggestion of a light moustache. Her eyelids suddenly
stiffen, the eyes narrow, a flash from the side: an elegant
little French four-seater limousine rolls up, with yellow
wheels, pleasingly curved bonnet and back end. Inside, bolt
upright, despite the danger of hitting their heads, somewhat
too close together, sit three German uniforms, field grey,
black and silver, with a civilian at the wheel. Four identical
jawlines, identical spines. For a second, their gaze shifts to
the corner of their eyes, a quick probe to the left, then fixed
straight ahead again. Then you see, on the back, a number
with, before it, the letters "POL". In a broad, gentle arc,
the car steadily accelerates across the chaotic carrefour in
front of the Chambre des députés, turning into the steep
shady street after Place Bourbon(?). Taking no notice of the
traffic streaming towards it from all angles – embankment,
bridge, boulevard – a long cart pulled by white-maned heavy
horses, a rickety wagon with gas cylinders tucked to one
side behind the cab. The trafficator – a red hand, cut from
a piece of board – flips out to the left. The wooden setts
have been partially replaced with cobblestones, further piles
of which restrict the pavement in front of the Chambre.
Lifeless tram tracks. The wall in front of the temple façade –
Défense d'uriner – has bouquets of spikes running along

the top. A blossoming cherry tree and the mature, faded statue of Calvin(?), seated with legs gingerly crossed and a bare, oblong skull. Half-eaten by the wind, the swastika flag on the top of the pediment flaps in constant ecstasy. In place of an acroterion, an abandoned wooden shelter for anti-aircraft guns.

Autre...

The Métro. Seated opposite one another – knee to knee in the crush on the narrow, low seats – are a rifleman and an Oriental girl. His mate looks at her from the side. They cannot take their eyes off her, now and again fingering their chins or the edge of their caps.

She sits stock-still, her long spine glued to the back of the seat, in a dark blue coat with an upturned collar. Her thin black hair is almost entirely concealed by a patterned blue headscarf, which drapes down onto her coat at the back and the side. A silver crescent the size of a five-mark piece is attached to her forehead. She keeps her head bowed, with not so much as a flutter from her long eyelashes. Pronounced bags under the eyes, casting heavy shadows. The nose a long, narrow ridge, protruding to a sudden sharp bend, then curving keenly down, almost inwards; the flexible, clearly defined sides of her nose. The cheeks are hollow, very long, the cheekbones pronounced. Even the upper lip is unduly long, with the shadow of a moustache. The protruding, wet lower lip – always edging forward, smacking – and a savage bitterness to the corners of her mouth evoke the noble features of a camel. The long, firm chin. The neck seems scrawny, the larynx in constant motion.

At one point, a sinewy little brown hand, with pointy, varnished fingernails, moves to her nose; her whole forehead subsides into irregular, wide, bulging wrinkles.

The soldiers cannot account for her appearance. From her legs they catch a flash of browny-bronze; their bareness seems particularly European: socks rolled down to the ankles, in white, sandal-like slippers.

They have reached their stop. Outside on the platform: "Nice girls here… But what kind of Jewish shiksa was that?"

"Nah. Turkish more like."

"Noo… they're smaller. That was probably some old Arabian mare. Black Death of Aleppo."

"What? She weren't even thirty."

"Come off it! Looking like that? Past it she was. All shrivelled up."

"She weren't that bad… I don't know about you, Maxe, but I wouldn't say no to a bit of 'racial defilement'…"

"I'm with you there. Get that across your knob…"

"Right. That's enough of that. How do you bloody get out of here?"

Moonlight idyll in Central Europe

(A guest speaker from the Reich said that Paris today is nothing more than a provincial European city. "There is no longer any need to approach it with reverence.")

Blackout. There is an eleven-o'clock curfew for Parisians. Only occupying forces are left on the streets, which are deathly quiet. Military boots, solitary or in groups, the odd civilian scooting past, the brim of his hat pulled down low. A breezy night, some big marauding clouds float past at a reasonable height, a burnt-brownish colour. In a patchy bank of cloud, scattered spots of moonlight. Further south, in the rough direction of the Dôme des Invalides, a searchlight shoots up, fixing on a low, ragged cloud, which appears to stop, stretching out paws anew. The searchlight, cut off from the ground, dies away in a fraction of a second.

Rue de la Paix. The glaring white eye of a lamp blinks on; two men in capes. "Votre laissez-passer, s'il vous plaît." "Bien, merci beaucoup…" A faint click of heels. From a doorway on the next street corner, a weak blue torch makes timid appeals to the chests of passers-by. A soft, deep voice: "Monsieur, voulez-vous… on va monter tous les deux." A civilian, in a tight, fur-trimmed coat, answers with the blinding white beam of a powerful cylinder torch (a "Lichtdolch"), which he shines in her face for a considerable time.

Outside "Maxim's", a row of horse-drawn cabs, with motionless nags and drivers in silhouette… In front of a hotel in Avenue de l'Opéra, a man swaps a cab for a motorcar, hampered in the process by his cavalry sabre. A gentle squeaking, rocking, jangling, the chafing of silk. The hushed, smooth approach of a long limousine. Its grainy grey paintwork almost completely soaks up the moonlight.

For a moment, the moon, with its tattered wet face, is free, and makes a dash for the nearest cloud. Outside the Ritz, the front of which lies in shadow, two flashing glints of metal: the steel helmets of the two soldiers on sentry duty, motionless, their legs rigidly apart; slouching in the middle, a moonstruck little NCO with an overlarge holster. Suddenly: ssshhh, clump, trump – present arms! The dazzling mirror of the square has suddenly given birth to a little silvery, wraithlike figure, gliding up to the hotel entrance. Some shadowy ancient reefs: piles of snow which have yet to be cleared… An air corporal crosses with a girl, finding it hard to keep pace with the moon's course along the Avenue de l'Opéra. The girl looks up at the moon, stifling a throaty cough. They are swallowed up in the shadows of a narrow side street; only the sound of boots is left behind.

The moon plunges into the cloud, and the illuminated side of the street is blotted out. Place de la Concorde. The edges are almost erased by the moonlight. The bare trees, railings in the Tuileries Garden flicker unbearably. The gentle ripple of flags on the admiralty building. Old piles of snow, glistening puddles, ruffled by the wind, road studs; feet hesitate towards shadows cast by street lamps, stumbling off shallow kerbs. In the darkest shadows outside the admiralty, two young sailors with a cumbersome, rattling hamper. Gingerly, a car curls across the square, heading for a forlorn civilian with wet feet: "Pouvez... vous... me dire... où: 'Chez elle'... Lucienne Boyer*..." "It's all right, Lieutenant. You can speak German."

Rue [de] Rivoli, the shadows three times as dark under the arcades. A couple of steps from the entrance to a hotel, guarded by sentries: the silent, motionless form of a couple kissing. Far beyond, a sharp explosion of giggling ricochets around the arches. Then here they come, marching along, the legs in the middle, in silk stockings, flying highest: left, two, three, four... – You know, I really am most frightfully squiffy, but I can march a damn sight better than you: left, two, three...

The pale Pont Royal, verging on the invisible, rises up sharply from the embankment, out of ivory marble and ashen snow. But there is gold there, too. A gentle old forgotten glow in the cold of the stone and the moon, yet fingers are too short, nails too thick, to feel it. The smell of burning, of ash and moon, of scorched, ground stone, is something for the spirits to discern...

Two cigars come strolling over the crest of the bridge. "She was having a laugh... There was the tip, something for the femme de chambre, then she went and drank three-quarters of a bottle of champagne... I won't be doing that again. Blimey." "That's the last thing on my mind... I've got to get wool for my mother. Last week, it was slippers for my brother-in-law. It's costing me a fortune, I can tell you. Families. Honestly. May as well throw myself in the river right now."

---

* Lucienne Boyer (1901–1983), a popular French singer.

Dimanche – Île Saint-Louis, April

Looking west across the edge of the Pont Marie. Fluffy clouds in an overcast sky. A wall of rain and hail – plum-blue, with whitish streaks – rises up above the Palais de Justice. The air feels close; the scorching sun was just out. From the bridge, one can reach up into the branches of a large old plane tree rooted in the stone of the embankment which leans out over the river. It is covered in fresh glossy reddish-green leaves. Smaller young seed pods – yellow, crimson in places – alongside the old ones on their wizened threads. The stormy sky, purplish-blue, beyond.

The scraping, shuffling of all the feet on the bridge, the embankment. There is little talk. The boxes of the bouquinistes are all open, causing clots to form in the flow. The dealer stands out in the road to avoid being swept away. Tired family groups sit back-to-back on the low double benches in the midst of the throng. Adolescents, arms thrown along the tops of the benches, children, heads tipped back, watching the faces of those shuffling by. Perambulators with anaemic infants' faces, sound asleep, a drop of sweat on their foreheads.

The vast reeking halo which surrounds the conveniences, outside which those queueing stand with nostrils blocked. On the island side, a bâteau-lavoir, the hulls of three boats next to each other, long metal funnels – black and corroded with rust, held up with wires – sticking up as high as the railings on the bridge. On top are the drying-lofts, open to the elements. Through the wavy wire grating, one can see large off-white sheets, each one almost touching the next, stretched out side by side. At the waterline, underneath a roof of thick greenish glass, is the laundry itself; on weekdays, the whole rat-infested tub clatters and sways to the rhythm of the washing bats and constant chug-chug of steam pouring out of the flues. There is also a kind of floating veranda, with all manner of potted plants and flowerpots strung up on wires. On a cast-iron garden table, a cage belonging to a grey-blue parrot with a red head, which every other minute lets out an almighty squawk. Two large black dogs come out onto the veranda, looking up at the people passing along the embankment on the other side of the wall.

Three children, each smaller than the last, stand cheek by jowl on top of the wide parapet wall, beside an angler, who must have lifted them up there. The anglers sit in shallow boats fastened to buoys – soldered-up jerrycans – or coloured poles rammed into the riverbed.

Over by Saint-Gervais, only the merest hint of the house fronts can be seen through the flowering poplars. The countless yellow dashes of dangling catkins, already filled out on some trees with the saturating brown-red-green of new leaf. Broad cobbled slopes and steep steps lead down to the quays themselves. A thin, steaming layer of mud, left over from the floods, mixed with pollen, bud casings and plane-tree seeds, covers the stones, muffling every step. Underneath the first arch of the Pont Marie, freshly painted boats are drying on blocks of wood, bottoms uppermost. Iron rings have been set into the arch, the sides of the piers and the cutwaters pointing upstream; chains, frayed old ropes hang down into the water. The wreckage from a smashed, sunken pontoon blocks the way through. The water flows slowly, laboriously, in viscous, sinewy swirls. The empty niches in the piers of the bridge. The infinite rich variety of blackish, yellowy hues on the stones and the broad trunks of the plane trees, as if they, too, had been turned to stone.

MAY 1941

Rooftops – Quartier Saint-Germain

May – – 9 p.m. – The view from the hotel window: the sky quite out of reach, a misted opal, veiled, shrouded, loosely covered by a web. In the west, in which direction you can only look by twisting your neck and pressing your face against the glass, a fiery golden red, intensifying by the minute. All the way over in the south, sprawling flat-topped mountain ranges emerge, with a muted glow. A calm across the roof-tops, but the air above, where the clouds are, is still churning. A little chimney smoke hangs powerlessly in the air, unable to expand or expire into the sky. The roofs of a rambling old hotel with various courtyards, low-level extensions. Partly covered with zinc, protruding at regular intervals in thick, bulging ribs of off-white. Or matt, grey-blue slate, which offers the sunset no reflection at all. The mighty chimneys, of brick set with quarry-faced stone, in force, burgeoning across the whole breadth of the building, far above the ridge of the roof. Then a series of short clay chimney pots is unleashed, or a forest of dark rusty pipes with all manner of caps and cowls. The entire skyline – other rooftops jostle behind the hotel – bristles with hundreds of such pipe-heads and halberds. The roofs everywhere broken up, held back, turned into garrets, opened up by skylights, œils-de-bœuf, an inhabited, occupied space, a metropolis, a world of its own behind the screen of those great bare chimney walls. The thick canopy of trees which pervades certain courtyards provides a safe practicable base for the city's rooftop world. Individual chestnut trees – round in shape, their leaves fully unfurled – fill the courtyards as lungs fill a ribcage, a deep breath of air the lungs. A ponderous fat pigeon attempts to infiltrate the chestnut canopy. There are a few swallows about. They come together in a knot, before darting off into the empty street – for a second, the ear is overwhelmed by their shrill cries – and casting themselves to the four corners of the sky; you can still see some of them, above other parts of the city. – Beyond the forest of chimneys, the dome of Les Invalides rises up into the sky, lavishly chased with gold: dulled a thousandfold by wind and water, and yet a quite unreal golden gold. Vertical stripes, festooned with garlands and trophies in between. Only the curve of the cupola is visible, the drum concealed.

The fiery glow in the west has now caught on a large mass of cloud; it suddenly spreads across the untouchable sea of roofs, and individual chimneys, pipe metal, skylights, slates flame golden-red. Shortly before it disappeared, just for a moment the sun gained open water. Even at street level, tongues of luminous bronze pour down. The shoulders of an abbé, just crossing the street, turn gold.

Views across Paris – Île de France

Up in Montmorency. Thickets of young chestnut shoots, yet not so dense that one cannot see through, radiating out in bursting clumps, their bark silver-white, long hairs edging the thin young leaves. In between, scrubby young oaks, crisp, bulging leaves, coppery hues. Solitary oak trees bear their canopies above, the first frills of blossom and yellow leaf foaming in the wind. Wood being pilfered from the fracturing, fissuring earth, the hurried irregular blows of an axe. Faint woodsmoke nearby, but no scent on the wind.

A clearing. Les pervenches. Pale ferns, still curled up. The stalks of coppiced chestnut saplings cluster together. The edges of the copse, which lag behind, fill with wind, then slough it off, a cooing of doves the while. The plateau, naked, dissected, relinquished, [blank] half-effaced by a dazzling spring light which falls almost vertically to the ground. Lazy clouds drag their broad lilac-brown shadows behind them, often, it seems, coinciding with a hollow, [blank] a patch of woodland, slow to shift. The brightness still pale and wintry; seeing the shadows bearing down makes one shiver, while the bright-edged clouds give rise to a feeling of heat, a warm, steamy wind. The gasometers like hubs of darkness, in two groups, by the Gare du Nord and the Gare de l'Est, where there hangs a thick pall of sluggish, yellowy-grey smoke; another, closer, further west, towards Saint-Denis. Some lie unconscious, collapsed to the ground, inside their frames. Chimneys in even rows, most of them black, no smoke. A stretch of canal, a loop in the Seine, flashing like tin through the midday haze. Centre stage, the butte of Montmartre. It looks more rugged than when you see it from the city. The Sacré-Cœur – one cannot make out details, even tell the campanile from the central dome – draws most of the light. A cliff of glaring yellow marble, a frozen termite mound. The foot of the hill lies in shadow cast by the clouds, a sea of ink. One after the other, the terraces of houses which, heaped up, press against the church, go under. And now even the cupola turns grey, the tower dying away, deep blue flowing in behind. The reef of houses and church seems to subside, leaving only a dark wet bulwark [blank], the edges of which are already creeping up the hill, a wave in a sea of rooftops, on the far side of the Seine. One can clearly see factory buildings, houses below Montmartre, around Saint-Denis [blank]: concentrated around the road and rail junctions, bridges, their glass roofs flashing, firewalls shrill. The great city beyond that marble reef lies embedded in a soft haze, any detail concealed: gently undulating [blank] fields of rooftops [blank], endless, boundless, in each and every direction, spread out as far as the horizon across the hill, an endless sheet of dough, rolled, beaten out, baked to a stone.

In some places, the veil is thinner, the scab-like roofs coming clearly to the fore, rutted and scarred. Individual domes protrude: the Panthéon, compressed by the distance, dark as a mole, only visible thanks to the hill it sits on; and, boundless, with its golden glimmer, the dome of Les Invalides. That gold, the only real colour in the brilliant great carpet of light and shade; livelier, warmer [blank] than the garish flowers in the woods.

The hills – Vanves, Issy [blank] finally restrict – too late – the floundering, exhausted eye.

Blitzmädchen[*]

With barely a sound, the commuter train is sucked along a straight section of track, out of the city. The banlieue slips past. The door, the area for standing passengers and luggage in the middle of the carriage. They congregate around the gleaming handrail, feet apart, although the movement of the train is smooth and even. Young things, not unattractive, some of them. Everyone talking at once, their clamorous voices all the same: high-pitched and monotone, the odd Bavarian accent providing the only splash of colour. A wave of laughter [blank] They all have the same dull, light-brown

---

[*] Literally 'lightning girls', Blitzmädchen was the slang term for girls and young women who served as auxiliaries with the Wehrmacht during the war.

hair, jarring with the poisonous yellow piping on their caps. Downy childlike cheeks, their faces, mostly, an explosion of large pale freckles. The chatter lacks any real vibrancy, as if a birdcage had been hung from the ceiling of the carriage. It is not so much the foreign tongue, seemingly, as the tonal colour – a dull grey, aquamarine – which prevents the voices from carrying. Air, metal and wood do not conduct.

There are solely French sitting on the seats, in silence. Saturday afternoon, after hours: muggy and close. The few minutes between each of the suburban stations drag on interminably. Arched brows, eyes frozen wide open, lines etched on foreheads, at the corner of the mouth, one woman suppressing a nervous gulp. Everyone's gaze, as if spellbound, fixed on the girls (not on individual faces: their hair, some impossible feature of their uniform), blotted out, leached with horror, revulsion, and yet with a kind of voracity. Their fervent, utter addiction and the boundless forbearance of that deep-seated hatred; hatred is not the word. A young man in a speckled trench coat: a narrow mouth that would forever spit them out, the nostrils constrict in offence, yet – playing with fire – he cannot take his eyes off them. A woman in black, her face slightly veiled, a dampness about the eyes. The dark-red, enamelled mouth – crispée – drawn in slightly, the varnish holding it in place. No noticeable breath. She would so love to close her eyes, turn her head away, but cannot. The withered neck, the odd grey curl. She has reached her stop – a quiet, brutally clipped *"pardon"*, purged of any association. The girls are quick to make space, almost dividing in two. The woman is small, seems to be limping slightly, her movements smudged. – A big man with no neck, oozing over his collar in all directions. He nods off for a few seconds, before his eyes, large, flecked with light blue, open again.

Some of the girls are tired from being on their feet and, swiftly and silently, distribute themselves around the various empty seats. One drops down with military aplomb, dust and red-faced embarrassment the result. No reaction from any of the other faces; some people even take their eyes off her for a moment. A few more gaffes like that might ease the tension. But it is the girls', in essence, entirely unobjectionable behaviour which really sickens the French. – In isolation, the faces suddenly age, the necks stiffen, a touch lopsided, feeling the burden of a muggy afternoon. They try to keep half an ear on everyone else's conversations, chipping in from a distance, most of the interjections passing unheard. Their legs tightly pressed together in those thin black crêpe stockings; they don't look around.

On the Terrasse at Saint-Germain, the mob breaks up completely; individual couples. Swallows dart above their heads. Lone women at work in the overgrown gardens running down to the Seine, bent double or shuffling around on their knees. Great beds of strawberries. Faded cherry trees with hardly any clumps of green fruit. Behind the wall of surging lime trees, buffeted about by the wind, a confusion of cuckoos' voices, countless blackbirds(?), rise and fall. The damp in the air is far-reaching; it might rain any minute. A cumbersome great transport plane skims over the thronging woods, the blanket of cloud hanging low.

They march along a bluish asphalt avenue through the woods. A gang of adolescents, on racing bikes, leaning down over the handlebars, whizz past within a hair's breadth: a whistle, then the pull of the airstream behind them. In a patch of woodland full of young trees as thick as your finger, a great golden blaze, smokeless, rises against the backdrop of green, a woodman alongside; the delicious crackle.

The park wall

It runs for miles alongside the high road. [blank] There is a crest to begin with, a little roof made of tiles angled against each other which glow in the sun. Scabrous with golden-brown lichen. Only traces of render, which will soon fall off altogether. It reveals how it was made: using roundish, undressed field stones, most of them about the size of your head, with lots of mortar in between, which rushes round, gripping them with thick gnarled fingers. Weather-worn in places, crumbling away, the dull, round faces of stone float one above the other, deep dark gorges in between, the inside of the wall clinging on to them. The bottom immersed in the grim forest of stinging nettles rising up out of the ditch by the side of the road.

Suddenly there is a mown patch; the sickle came just below the face of the stones, a yellowy-green carpet falling gently away into the ditch. A sack of cut grass, half-full, with a loose gaping mouth, a metal flask beside it, grey enamel. A band of stocky thistles outstrips the battered [blank] nettles [blank] The wall loses its tiled roof, the bald weather-worn tops of the stones lying exposed, some missing, then whole sections have been prised out, the wall dropping in height; one can look over, standing on the bulging ridges of asphalt in the road.

Beyond the wall, nothing but forest: dense, dark, taller than the sun, which only throws the occasional narrow jerky glance through the tops of the trees. The dry lustreless green of the elms: holes in every leaf, many riddled with them; if you stand still, you can hear a low, steady rustling, a trickling down: caterpillars eating. Stiff and straight, the grubs fall off towards the wall; suddenly caught, they float, swinging on their invisible threads above the warm stone.

A clearing – the sky almost comes down as far as the top of the wall, with hefty great clouds, but the midday haze holds it back, keeping it behind the sun. Individual oak trees, awash with frizzy new leaf, stretch their regal branches. Unhurried circling crows.

Dense forest again. A hole in the ground, as if a cannon-ball had smashed through. One can see how thick the wall is, and what it's made up of: yellowish mortar, either in wide streams or disintegrated into pillows of sand; soil; tangled roots. An old woman comes cautiously through, on all fours, glancing up the road; behind her, on a length of cord, she tugs at a recalcitrant bundle of sticks. The weathered crest along the top of the wall is now green: tufts of grass, young oak shoots, with coppery leaves, dead-nettles with blooming bonnets of blue, white.

Now the forest retreats, leaving only the brewing, clouded sky behind the wall, above which the warm air quivers. One can now see how densely packed it is, some clouds heaving along leaden bellies. A gateway – two pillars made up of only a few soft blocks of stone, with bulky mouldings, the arch missing; stonecrop sprawling out of a tin-glaze pot. The view through the pillars is across broad pastureland bright with flowers. Clumps of mighty chestnut trees (what's left of an old avenue), round, lush, resplendent with flower-spikes, stagger towards a radiant white country house. Single-storey, with a long curved roof, Lombardy poplars with the tops lopped off, three times as tall. The forest lies just beyond like a great mound of leaves, upon which large puddles of shadow have begun to appear.

Suddenly, the wall breaks off completely, to be replaced by a ragged hawthorn hedge, criss-crossed by barbed wire with varying degrees of rust. Hefty brown forms behind, which slowly move, a pair of horns appears, twitching ears. Cows huddle in the strip of shade offered by the hedge. The wall reappears out of the ground, once more wearing its tiled crown and covered in even, grey plaster. On the wires [breaks off]

JUNE, JULY 1941

Il fait lourd

The walls seem to exude a heavy grey gas. Like somebody who ran out of breath long ago, but is still breathing out, through gritted teeth, their temples throbbing. As if something in the structure of the stone had suddenly given way, enlarging the pores. This mingles with the fumes of German leaded petrol; a veritable blue fog hangs across the Place Vendôme, swallowing up the intrinsic design of the house front opposite.

The [blank] sky hangs listlessly, [blank] the brooding clouds unleashed, in tatters, across the rooftops. The chimneys look particularly weather-worn and threatened, the smoke refusing to detach itself from them. At the bottom of the street, the sky is streaked with peacock blue, the only colour which the haze cannot repress. The pigeons flap sluggishly, as if their wings were encased in iron. Clothes stick to the body, the eyeballs ache. Air blows cool from every doorway, every side street. The gutter flooded as usual, the water coursing by inexplicably fast, noiseless and clear, the surface lightly rippled. Everywhere you look, you are confronted by dog dirt, tortured asthmatic scraps. An old, greyish-white, pug-like dog, the colour of a dapple grey, with pink rims around its lashless eyes, coughing, sneezing, vomiting with a deep satisfaction. Horses wait in front of a removal van, with bags, buckets made out of canvas pulled over their mouths, right up under their eyes, the bottoms dark with moisture; they try to shake them off. Beside them, on the pavement, a pressed bale of straw. They constantly shift their weight from leg to leg.

Avenue de l'Opéra. The grey expanse of parked Wehrmacht cars. The guard outside the Kommandatur with a streaming forehead, paper-white; hopefully he won't keel over. A towering SS lieutenant with an apathetic flaxen-haired woman, half the size of him. Bandy legs, huge great backside, a long nose on a suntanned face. She speaks softly, him leaning over her with one shoulder. Squaddies, probably discharged reservists, in unbelievably ill-fitting uniforms, trousers sagging at the seat, minus bayonets, in lace-up boots. Incredibly bruised and bitter Silesian guttural. Their arms so full of packages they can only nod in greeting. Window displays: colis for detainees, cockades made of red, white and blue paper stuck to the glass, a tower of large pretend packages. German travel office: pictures of the Wehrmacht with parallel text; motorboats with short masts and great bow waves in front. A sky full of vapour trails, a heavy anti-aircraft gun firing at night, the billowing white bloom of muzzle flash at the end of the long thin barrel. From the world of culture: the Berlin State Opera in Paris. The startling face of a prima donna blazes white, three-quarters hidden by flowers and furs. – The last member of staff comes out, a bilingual youth in a blue blazer, the wetted parting to his hair glossy black. Slowly, looking up and down the street, he pulls the sparkling nickel-and-glass door to, locking it with a small shiny key, turning it once, twice, three times, like clockwork. Crossing the street at an angle, following an outstretched finger, three German office women head towards a crocheted blouse: the price has gone up again.

Two adolescent girls with thick mops of hair, round faces, stroll along with an alluring ease, showing off their legs. The lopsided [blank] hurried gait of many of the women. With some it is a hobbling blur. Faces sucked out from within, the lips, cheeks drawn in. One girl's fragments completely for a moment when she anxiously pats the side of her coiffure. The path of her forehead stirred up, cast adrift, the eyes wide. The cheek comes away from the mouth, staying to one side, too heavy for a face which can no longer hold it. The mouth is keen to burrow away inside, its corners suggesting a laugh. Yet the lower lip demurs and slips down, as if athirst.

She tries to read something in the gleaming brown skin covering the forehead of an approaching young man; it goes well with the blue jacket he's wearing. Nothing. The eyes, shards of blue, yet not as blue as the jacket, flash past her. But when a German comes along, the eyelids suddenly tighten again, the lips close, the breath spare. Looking up, at an angle [blank], often through a black veil, her gaze clings to him, enveloping him with a kind of voracity, extracting all.

A queue outside a patisserie, snaking round the next corner, into a side street. An administrative air officer right in the middle, moments from losing his temper. He seems to have sneaked in: the little women push and shove him. He makes an obliging attempt to draw in his bottom and his belly, but finds no favour. Near him is a senior Red Cross nurse, her sou'wester a rallying cry, mute and blue, in the battle of hips. Inside, a serving girl's splayed skinny fingers, with long nails, continuously tying up bundles of cakes; she is methodical in varying which fingertips she uses, pour ne pas trop les abîmer. Right next to the queue, at a little table which judders from constantly being knocked, little ladies sip hot chocolate; it is only available twice a week between 3 and 4.

At the beginning of a narrow side street, somewhere up between the nearby chimneys, the sky is rent by a half-choked rasping sound: thunder, which then seems to move away, to burrow behind the clouds, while the volume increases. The pavilion of the Louvre, which marks an end to the street, suddenly lies behind a curtain of whitish streaks. The rain has arrived. In ferocious, almost targeted drops. They perforate the haze and the mugginess, rather than subduing them. On your nose, the roots of your hair. The men hunch their shoulders; the women have thin, largely yellow umbrellas. Then it dries up again. The slate roof [breaks off]

Memories of Rouen

In the south, steep hillsides border the town: completely undeveloped virgin meads, short wet flowerless grass. Towards the river the carpet tears on precipitous, almost vertical limestone cliffs. An onshore wind, suffused with rain. A couple of roaring trees bent inland, a white poplar, some sycamores, like in the foothills of the Alps; one can see them from the depths of the town, looking from the squares and embankments. Gnarled, long-fingered flints lie in the grass, their surface bone-white. Quarried pits, pale clay and loose limestone gravel. Only a cemetery heads on up the slope, a low red brick wall cutting a curved triangle out of it. From the young oaks and sycamores, dotted along the one main avenue, the wind stirs up brown, coppery hues; an autumnal effect.

The town grey, purple, hardly any brick red. Churches the colour of cobwebs. The green copper on the roof of the cathedral chancel. The bells of Saint-Ouen ring out, the sound seemingly coming from the nave, not soaring aloft. The towers stand mute the while, benumbed in their lacy stone mantles. Corpus Christi has been transferred to this Sunday. The bells stop without any echo, dropping down onto rooftops nearby. The cathedral's gros bourdon resumes, on its own, in slow arcs, but even this sound restricts, sub-terraneously; one cannot tell which of the two towers it is coming from. The devastated quarter between the cathedral and the river; seen from up here it condenses into a hand-breadth of charred tones. The outer walls of the covered market are still standing, one-storey, a long, repeating run of identical empty square windows. The west end of one chapel with a single great baie of tracery, a threshing-floor clean and tidy where the nave used to be. Walls of old half-timbered houses, vertical nut-brown stripes side by side. The embankments, extending into the debris zone, strewn with fresh yellow sand, still with no defined edge towards the water. Dark Sunday figurines inch slowly up- and downstream. The bridge, braced by new minium-red steel girders, still sags slightly. Further upstream a narrow temporary footbridge, just as bowed. The low-lying warehouses on the island look like they have been stove in by the sheer force, or the pull, of the blasts; collapsed. Roofs, still with their old tiles, hang down as far as the ground, into the elder bushes in the riverside gardens.

Further south, part of the "invasion fleet" (?) lies at anchor in the middle of the river, dark barges drawn together into a solid mass. Only a small section is missing from the spare simple framework of the new railway suspension bridge. The never-ending Seine retreats far to the west, downstream. Long, tall and even, a steep, darkly wooded bank traces its course along one side, disappearing into the haze between constricted gaps in the trees.

Saint-Cloud – Allée des Marnes

Midday cloud, which holds its own well into late afternoon, slowly drawing a veil over the hot bright sky. Wave after wave of thin haze shroud the sun, the edges of the clouds imperceptibly thickening, pushing back its rays. Not a breath of wind. The long avenue of chestnut trees, taillés en rideau, dropping gently down towards the Seine. At the end, above the grass, framed by the dark, almost chiselled walls of trees, one can see what looks like a parched field of shattered remains, dawning grey. Some larger pieces – triangles, trapezoids – stick out irregularly. Unless one looks closely, it merges with the greyish-purple base of the sky, in which one can see the faint tops of some clouds: a great section of the city taken over by enormous greyish-purple shadows of cloud.

The path leads right alongside the chestnut trunks; the centre of the avenue is meadow, with solitary tall, faded grasses and sparse little yellow flower heads, infiltrated in places by clumps of stinging nettles. It is criss-crossed by narrow, worn tracks, with no regard to the overall view, dogged little routes between the clusters of houses, gardens, which one can sense to the left and the right of the leafy park. Solitary encampments. On a low garden chair driven into the undulating meadow, a girl with a large, fleshy back in a pale dress. She is darning stockings, a whole pile of them, sheer slender casings spread across her knee. At her feet, almost invisible in the long grass, a young man; one can only hear his deep, constricted voice: he has laid his head, mouth, on the upper part of his brown arm. Low-slung perambulators have dropped anchor, plump crouching mothers dressed in black, in the shadow of the trees; a baby on a blanket, terribly small and still, its back glued to the ground. The helpless eyes, which only close in sleep, turned upwards towards the oppressive, motionless mountains of leaves, the hot, faceless, colourless sky. Another perambulator, covered with black oilcloth, brimming with grass and brushwood. Stooped figures, hurriedly cutting, tearing at the patch around them. Bent

over whirring bikes, with no bells, foresters glide towards the
city. Behind them lingers the delicious scent of red wine and
tobacco. One of them has lashed trunks as thick as your arm,
fresh with axe marks, across the handlebars onto the saddle,
an oscillating bundle of spears which protrudes, fore and aft,
for several feet. Others hurry on foot, shouldering scythes,
long-handled rakes, the "berace", the hollow cow's horn
with its whetstone, hanging from their hips. The chestnuts
have been cut back, beneath protruding corniced tops, into
a thin, almost transparent wall; they are largely formed of
ebony branches, but loosely clad in large leafy hands, the
thick impenetrable bank of leaves taking shape up above.

Sudden gaps: half a dozen trees missing. Sometimes
saplings step into the breach, translucent, with little leaves,
still a long way off the desired height, or the odd old lime
tree, which despite all the space seem to lack air and have
stopped growing. – In some of the rows of trees it is as
if the fervid birdcalls had been scrunched together by a
hand, reacting to the rise and fall of its pulse. Sometimes
the park on either side of the avenue seems to go on forever – long transverse avenues, their trees grown together
to form an arch, descend down gentle flanking slopes, the
ground appearing black, damp, untrodden; then it narrows
again, or disappears entirely – a trackbed encroaches into
the avenue, a railway line passing underneath. Behind a thin
curtain of trees, an ancient motorbike rattles and chugs, blue
asphalt coming into view. A wall made of pale field stones,
the outline of which quivers in the sun, makes space for a
square of garden – beanpoles, strawberry leaves trailing on

dry clods of earth. An open meadow between still banks of foliage seems other-worldly, to belong to a different environment completely. An almost imperceptible blue haze wafts around the rigid trees: smoke from a little fire which cannot find the sky.

A rond-point: the chestnuts do not lead all the way up; beyond, the dense screen gradually starts once more. The basin of a fountain brims with thick brown water. Old goldfish, scales missing, pink, off-white, floating in a criss-cross jumble like dead wood or swimming round in procession. Statues of Mercury, in pairs, at the junctions with the side avenues, skirt the worn edges of the lawns. Where the column transforms into the torso, a stone sash loops around into an enormous knot. The goddesses' breasts are too far apart, pointing in different directions. Some, in imitation, are made from stucco and exhibit broad, jagged cracks. The ones made of stone are draped in golden moss.

The final part of the avenue drops more sharply, towards an invisible flight of steps which leads down to the Seine. The smooth bodies of two vases dazzle. And the city is suddenly in [blank] It has consumed the great shadows cast by the clouds and now there unfold thousands of [blank] At the very front, glass roofs, firewalls and factory chimneys, the odd tall one among them, onto which smoke feebly hangs, and rows of blackened stumps, like upturned rakes. The façades of the buildings seem to confront the avenue, crosswise, the streets, which plunge deeper, almost submerged.

Summer, wind...

The façades along the Quai Bourbon on the north side of the Île Saint-Louis. [blank] The great bodies [blank] Only their tops and backs, turned towards the water, are still [blank] by light which, coming from afar, [blank] by many a wind, picks out every leaf in gold. The leaves gleam from within, like ripened fruit almost, not from a glossy outer skin. The soughing seems to get greater and greater. There are the myriad voices of the outer leaves, busily chattering all at once, an unending, heedless flurry; but the internal body of the tree also has a voice, without a single tongue, more an irregular breathing, sighing, bordering on song; and then often one limb is seized by a particular thrill; all the others drown it out, an incomprehensible age-old lament or a laugh which stirs up some ponderous phrase, with a metallic jangle. Sometimes a particular tree in the row wants to be exempt, to fall silent from within, but its leaves, intimately united with those of its neighbour, are constantly being infected, and continue to rustle. The air is filled with drifting catkin fluff from the poplars. The greyish-white down even floats across from the other side of the river, settling on the embankment wall before being blown off by the wind, which has driven great stocks of it behind the guard stones by the entrance gates, on the stepped pavement. A lot of grey still hangs in the trees. Domed foreheads and angular cheeks on the stone heads above the gateways [blank] silently doubles [blanks] the surging leaves. A yellow silk curtain, secured at one end, flails around in a window. As noise from the trees increases, it flaps about, a brisk rhythmic slapping, till it gets all twisted up. Most of the windows are open, seemingly into tall, sparsely furnished rooms. The fluff from the trees floats past the thin dark rectangles, the silence scored by the cries of swallows darting past. The grey-green limewashed façade of the final palais which fronts onto the little square at the western tip of the island: curving imperceptibly inwards, divided up by strips and narrow pilasters. The panes of glass in the windows criss-crossed over and over with lengths of tape. The corner quoins(?) both have, pressed in halfway up, like a waffle mould, the same oval relief: Hercules wielding a club above a centaur crushed to its knees.

Left, above the river [blank] Towards the east, the sound of bells is more sporadic, clashing and wilful. Notre-Dame now starts up, but even those bells, though carried by the wind, are held back somehow: the ear cannot have its fill. Out of the sun, cutting through, outstripping the sound of the bells, the roar of a solitary low [blank] aeroplane [blank] Reverberating against the shutters, window panes in the grey [blank] façade: a dry buzzing sound.

Coming back from Fontainebleau

With barely a sound, the train glides smoothly through the forest along a stretch of track as straight as a die. Blue smoke hangs above the clearings. Various shades of brown, browny-purple, among the oak leaf: little leaves, dry patches. Never-ending avenues, drenched in blue shadow; only the white sandy soil makes them [blank] come hurrying towards the railway embankment, for a moment sharing [blank] the leaves are suddenly [blank] like water that has been cut through. At the bottom of the western sky, a residual colour-less glow, which slowly consumes away. The night which has collected in the woods is in no hurry. The sky, translucent, tall and [blank] is still alive with its own colours. With a laboured beating of wings, a straggling line of great ravens battles along a steep leafy bank, as if they had spent the whole of the hot day flying around the edge of the huge forest.

In the compartment it is hot, thick with gloom. Faces radiate the glow of a hot day, gleaming red and brown. The luggage racks are loaded up to the ceiling: kitbags, gas masks, rifles. A compartment allocated to couriers, in a first-class carriage, in which German civilians and two Frenchwomen have established themselves. The soldiers sit next to one another, their backsides sunk into the plush, their knees, the thick fabric of their uniforms straining terribly across them, miles apart. One of them, by the window, receding [blank] hairline, bold aquiline nose, peers out, whistling. They only have one night in Paris – a city they do not know – before heading on to Saint-Malo tomorrow. Another, who later turns out to be a young student, a land surveyor, constantly comes into conflict with the Frenchwoman sitting next to him, due to his sweating, moaning and stretching out his legs. Despite repeated *"pardon"*s, he keeps on spreading out,

fidgeting, leaning back and forth in a vain attempt to get a
good look at his neighbour. She sits on the edge of the cushion, knees pointing towards the door, coolly presenting the
soldiers with the back of her loose red woollen dress, a mane
of golden blond hair: quite common in appearance, and yet
she doesn't particularly look like a "poule" to him. He feels
increasingly uncomfortable, as if one cheek were in the realm
of dance-class-like propriety, while the other is seared by a
lansquenet's thirst for action. ("We know how to behave"
versus "What's wrong with the tart?") In a voice which, due
to its sonorous register, is not suitably domestic, he recounts
what he's been up to, particular assignments, measuring
airstrips on the frontline, all infantry duties pushed to one
side for the past three months; the French have been getting a
bit cocky again, saw off the Russians in three weeks, etc. etc.
Participation on the part of the German civilians – two of
the three men wear spectacles, the girl, who has no bosom,
is in a sulk – is very slight, spasmodic. The man he spends
most of his time talking to is inhibited by the fact that the
soldier has not recognized him as a lieutenant on leave. – The
lack of resonance, the unliberated, insensible masculinity, a
victor's conceitedness, and the hot, tight collar on his uniform
give the soldier's words a threatening edge, shredding the
sentences in his mouth. The Frenchwomen's companions
out in the corridor, sporty young men in short-sleeved pull-
overs clutching bathing gear, keep casting concerned looks
into the darkened compartment, towards the gleaming
copper head of the soldier. ("Est-il ivre ou non?") – It is
not any easier for the other Frenchwoman, on the edge of

the cushion next to the corridor: she has to withstand the attention of the three German civilians, doubly oppressive with her not saying anything. The one sitting directly opposite, battling against the gathering darkness, fixes a steady gaze on her, pale-blue little goggle eyes behind thick lenses. Along with the nervous movements of his hands, large, and covered in distended veins. His neighbour affords her the occasional short reprieve by looking out the window and giving a lesson on the prevailing topography. He then issues short communiqués: "We're now approaching the Seine"… "Melun must be over there". But when his compatriots, coming round from their reveries, react, the net of his rapacious gaze [blank] is drawn ever more fervently, more tightly over its quarry. They cannot talk to him any more; he is vexatious, brusque, or does not reply at all. His prey has steadily buttoned her grey silk(?) blouse up to the neck, and put a man's jacket, borrowed from one of her companions, over the top. She forcefully lays her head against the headrest and tries to sleep. At which the three opposite, crossing their legs, move on to a completely unfettered examination. Her eyelids pull apart, destroying her brow. She gnaws at the dry scarlet red of her upper lip, which is a little too short; the nostrils contract. She is passed a cigarette from outside. Then, protected by a cautious hand, a little red flame, bent by the wind. The three companions forget about their own lighters until it is too late. – When the train speeds along between the walls of trees, tall and dark, her face against the headrest becomes a mere oval of golden brown [blank] Forest clearings, river fords, the sky:

all are drawn deep into the carriage window, highlighted in a mother-of-pearl reflection, heightened by the silver shimmer of mild perspiration. – Two small honey-yellow lights on the ceiling flick on for a moment, as if someone were trying them out. One of the soldiers stands up, groaning at various points. The Frenchwomen's pale sandals disappear under the seat like mice, as his heavy barge-like boots begin to head towards the door.

The train has now left the forest behind and, with ever-increasing speed, crosses a broad fertile plain: cornfields stretch as far as the eye can see, revealing that night has indeed gained the ascendancy. Almost all colour has drained away; only the fields of barley and oats still hold on to a silvery-white glow and the sky a suggestion of pink and emerald green. A screen of incredibly fine greyish-purple dust seems to be advancing at pace from the horizon, saturating the spent sky, and expunging one strip of field or woodland after another. The windows float like opalescent rectangles, rapidly growing dim, in a compartment which is now almost completely dark.

The dense motionless backs of dark chestnut avenues edge through the standing corn, their gigantic forms suddenly appearing by the railway. The outline of an old haystack against the sky, its steep pointed top leaning to one side. Suddenly the moon appears, first in the right-, then the left-hand window, still a dull reddish colour, not quite full, a piece of honeycomb consumed almost by the sky, now a gleaming shield, wrought from silver and copper. The light, which intensifies minute by minute, seems to stream from it in pulses. – A tower-like industrial plant; above the thick forest of chimneys there floats a motionless great conifer-shaped cloud of smoke. La banlieue.

Pleasure boat

A dull morning, the sky stuffed full of sluggish clouds, beginning just above the roof of the admiralty building. The Sacré-Cœur a smoking cone behind curtains of rain, which slowly close in around it. Any minute now the first drops will break upon the leaves of the trees in the Tuileries, hard and grey from the hot, airless night which waited in vain for the storm.

Faint twittering and tootling floats across the water, from underneath the bridge. Half-obscured by the arch, hard by the retaining wall, a little pleasure steamer full of soldiers in grey; an approaching train of barges has to be let past. A grey awning has been stretched across the upper deck, a narrow funnel protruding only a couple of hand's widths above. The soldiers sit knee to knee, hands on thighs; one cannot hear any conversation, their faces trained on the embankment wall. The stone seems soft, spongy; huge iron rings have been driven into it; the mouth of an égout, cemented round, gushes silently. Above, the pot-bellied posts along the balustrade and the sky bedecked with plane-tree pods. – In the stern, tightly framed by the braid of NCOs, a few nurses, with hunched backs. A stewardess in white linen, apparently selling cigarettes, fights her way through the abattis of legs and boots. A large sailor's hat with a red bobble sits perched at an angle atop her dark blond mane of hair. Her slim, nimble waist, her protruding slender hips are the only things to draw the eye. An adolescent crew in blue sailor suits practise gymnastics along the handrail; the decks are too crowded.

Finally, one spots the band. Four pallid hired civilians on rickety garden chairs, tucked away in a cramped corner between the bridge and the railings, a saxophone player among them. The long golden-brown toe of his boot, which sticks out over the deck, keeps time. He looks past his large nose at the people leaning towards him across the railings on the bridge. His lean jaw is mercilessly clean-shaven, the pale, firm, bulging cheeks above working tirelessly. – The steamer has a boat in tow, the back of which lies deep in the water under the weight of three motionless French policemen.

Windy night

Woken by frenzied rattling and flapping. The wind running amok outside; the window canopies in alarm. They rear up like animals trying to break free or fly away, up and down in their rigid frames, reaching a fever pitch of babbling and spluttering. In addition, there are the creaking hinges of a shutter, swinging helplessly yet solemnly between window and wall, and the swooshing and flapping of heavy satin curtains. Loose plumes are drawn diagonally across the street, pouring out of the [one word illegible] dark forest of quietly roaring flues.

A great grey cloud bank in tatters, torn apart by the force of the air. The sections right at the bottom overtake those above, the base floating away from the top. Even higher up, great streaming racks of cloud, heading west, almost in the opposite direction, before they disintegrate, the edges streaked by dying moonlight.

The surface of the street lies dry and grey, as yet untouched by rain. Two yawning policemen, idly puffing away, their caps pushed back, look up at the cloud-drift, their short jackets rolled up under their arms. It is still oppressive down there, the heat rising from the very grain of the stones. Then the thin silvery sound of two, three clocks striking in the building opposite. On the fifth floor, a silent figure in black silk briefly pushes open the shutters, the through-draught leading the eye into tall, sparsely furnished rooms. A sliver of gleaming parquet floor, with pewter and fine pottery in an oak dresser. At the back, in an open window, a hazy, greyish-purple patch of courtyard. There must be a large garden somewhere nearby. Buried deep in the leaves, two pigeons coo incessantly. Calm and soothing, and yet their voices are unremittingly gasping and urgent. [blank] it sounds like the roar of wild animals. – Then the crescent moon appears for a moment among the driving clouds: one cusp curling over, the other smouldering, as if in frantic flight.

Propaganda

The grand terrace above the Chevreuse Valley (Robinson, [Hôtel] L'Ermitage) teeming with people, soldiers and civilians, ladies, spindly bottlenecks, cigarette smoke rising straight up into the sky. Deathly silence, save for a faint click and whirr. Spots of golden-yellow light, on a tableau of glasses, flower arrangements, potted bay trees, screwed-up or lowered eyes: huge spotlights have been rigged up, along with the film cameras. Lean grey-haired French workmen fiddle with them, standing on chairs, straddling flower beds, in cotton-soled shoes. A pack of cameramen, military and civilian, constantly bumping into them, taking aim with screwed-up eyes, cameras against well-fed cheeks. Soon they'll be whirring off into the evening landscape, training their eye on that little chateau by the Seine, just within reach, the size of a thumbnail, standing in its own gardens; or they'll surprise tables where a conversation was beginning to blossom, capturing the lowered jaw, a gracious smile; or tap the mood of the great trees which shade the terrace. Sycamores and faded lime trees, the tops of which still gleam gold in the evening sun.

Always the same face: the afflatitious, musical brow, long swept-back hair, sometimes slightly greying. A blossoming, ruddy, yet still agile embonpoint. Soft skin which, wrapped in a cravat, luxuriates into a double chin. Horn-rimmed spectacles.

Then a solo violin starts up; the spotlights pick out a stage. A little corporal with a thatch of wavy blond hair which has escaped the once-over by the company sergeant major. Behind him, the accompaniment of a French jazz band, half lost in the shade of the trees, dressed in loose blue and white flannel; somewhat swollen faces. He flings back his curls, clomps with his boot. He finishes, thanking the weary ripple of applause with a click of the heels, a German salute. He then wheels into the darkness, towards the musicians, the spotlight not following him; he is about to shake hands with the band, but they are all busy with their music, instruments etc.

One of the cameramen is a private; stepping to one side to resolve a technical issue, he takes his camera apart, away from the light and lenses, on a bare table, paying no heed to a [blank] podgy little major with a huge duelling scar across his chin.

"Garsong!... Garsssong!... Bloody hell, a man could die of thirst here. Garssong!"

Eventually, the cameraman decides to respond to the parched cries. Taking off his spectacles and rubbing them with a handkerchief, he amiably asks, in a husky, pitch-perfect voice: "What can I get for you, Major?"

"Always bloody cables everywhere. Who are this lot?"

"Propaganda division, from military command, Major. Social evening."

"Huh. There's quite a few of them."

"You haven't seen the half of it. There's a whole load more in the ballroom. They've got two bands..."

"And you're what, filming it for the newsreel or something? Planning on showing troops at the front an enthralling picture of this important work in Paris? Give the old morale a boost, eh?"

"No, Major. This is for the archive."

"Marvellous. And then another lot will go and spend a year filming the work of the archive, in painstaking detail. Right: off you go now and get the waiter over here."

Le rendez-vous manqué – the displaced victor

"He" waits outside the Chambre des députés. A sultry late afternoon in high summer, colours washed out, not a breath of air, and leaden overcast skies. He dabs constantly at his temples with a wad of handkerchief, runs his fingers around his collar. Can't really remember the girl any more. The legs of his trousers seem too short; he is wearing lace-up summer shoes with thin soles, which squeak terribly. The toes are already white with dust. What should he do with his hands? Tuck them behind his back? That makes your head and neck stick out too much. Put them in your pockets and they won't be able to keep still. This is always something of a stumbling block with him. What should he do? – He really sticks out. The traffic policeman on the bridge keeps a close eye on him, even amid the frenzied whirl of cyclists; the other two, entrenched all the way down on the embankment under the plane trees, have their round brown faces fixed on him; he cannot tell their expression.

The columns across the front of the Chambre a brownish grey, the mouldings thick with dust. A white cardboard
"V" has been wedged into the tympanum. "La Campagne
triomphale des v." Victoire. Victoria. The large banner –
"Germany wins on all fronts" – which used to hang across
the colonnade has been missing since the morning. The
long gleaming silver skulls of Calvin, Colbert etc. that keep
watch in front of the steps on commodious thrones, scrolls,
books pressed against their shapely thighs. One wears the
expression of an old mastiff, black spots above the eyes. The
fenced-off corner – "Défense d'uriner." – The bouquets of
spikes along the crest of the wall. He is the only person
scuffing the thin soles of his shoes against the pale wide
pavement while he is waiting. The solitary passers-by hurry
past, short of time.

There is a pale shadow about his legs – the clouded sky
gives off a brilliant orangey-grey light. Towards the Rue de
Bourgogne, the pavement slopes away, constantly drawing
him towards the coping on the wall, and making him col-
lide with people coming the other way. It is still much too
early, at least according to his watch. Somewhere behind
the warm great mass of buildings, there is the sound of a
solitary sleepy bell, like from a village church – it should
be a quarter past. He presses his wristwatch to his ear – the
metal is hot and slippery.

The shapeless square in front of the Chambre, which rises
up towards the bridge, formed out of the junction of the
Quai d'Orsay and the Boulevard Saint-Germain, into which,
leading up out of the depths of the Quartier Saint-Germain,

the Rue de Bourgogne comes barging in. Loose sand left over from the recent roadworks (the tarmacadam was replaced with cobblestones); scorched, ground-up elm leaves.

Dusky brutes

Colonial troops on a Sunday pass. Evidently they are only allowed to frequent parts of the city where the possibility of meeting members of the German military is slight. The deserted embankments of the Île Saint-Louis on a Sunday, the hypnotic soughing of the poplars. Three come scuffing along, well spread out, in heavy hobnail boots, cigarette ends hanging from their mouths, hands buried in the pockets of their vast baggy trousers. Of their grey-green uniforms, only their caps, with deep furrows and pointed ends, seem to be new; coats and trousers hang off them, faded. There is no talk between them; the only sound in their ears is that of their boots. Only one, the shortest among them, with the wayward puttees, is a true frizzy-haired negro. He wears dark green glasses [blank]

Perhaps they are from the hospital; perhaps this is their first trip out into the city since they dragged the Germans out of the trees last summer. Their boots seem too heavy for them. The whiteness of their eyes and teeth, the purplish-brown of their hands and faces, are strangely intense when set off against the dull black trunks of the poplars, the muted grey and yellow ochre of the buildings, behind. The shutters on the big, tall windows are nearly all closed; the interiors seem fixed behind their slatted grates, even more distant and inaccessible than behind bare walls. When the shutters are pushed open, a dark, bluff, silent room peers out, the seams of heavy curtains tirelessly sweeping the windowsill. The heads above the doorways today resemble empty seashells blinded with lime, with festoons of fruit like blistered batter. High up in the breeze, between the flowerpots on a narrow balcony which runs across the whole width of the building, there stands a young couple. He sways in the doorway, looking over the trees, towards the embankment; a long white neck in an open shirt collar. She has her feet close together, solid elbows on the balcony railing, her head propped up in her hands. Her plump cheeks yield upwards, encroaching upon her eyes.

Her narrowed gaze is fixed somewhere between the soldiers, and does not follow them as they pass. The concierge, seated on a wicker stool, his feet in slippers, leaves his outstretched legs sticking out as the soldiers' boots trudge past. His little daughter, dressed up in her Sunday best, a pink outfit with a large yellow bonnet, is skipping with a rope. The backs of the anglers rigid in their shallow coloured boats. There is no end to what they have with them: camp stools, fitted fish tanks, dozens of pots and boxes. – Naked boys jumping into the green water from the steps.

The soldiers walk progressively slower, gradually edging their way towards the Pont Marie. On the other side is the lure of the cramped, dingy bistros of the Quartier Saint-Paul, somewhere they are perhaps not allowed to set foot. Their white eyes roll towards the edge of the bridge, back into the grey smoking half-light beneath the poplars. A girl walks briskly towards them, in clattering shoes; her breasts, in an airy blouse, wig-wag at every step. Another pair of soldiers, in scarlet red fezzes, slowly follow her at a distance, stopping at the top of the bridge. They are dressed in the same grey-green; one of them also has a thin crumpled coat, which hangs down to the backs of his knees. The vivid red colour above the central pier of the bridge is entirely on its own. The cloudy sky, the grey limestone, the slate, the pallid chimneys have no objections. Like blowing on a hot coal in fine grey ash. It is only among the mountainous slate of the Hôtel de Ville, the steep conical roof above the [blank] of the summery leaves [blank] that there is an inexplicable reddish-brown glow.

Out along the river...

A sultry summer afternoon, no wind whatsoever. Elongated, disembodied clouds, like bright white smears of mucus, stretching, spinning out, indiscernibly. The blue of the sky in between seems dull, robbed of its sheen, like faded satin. The branch of the river seems stationary, the marbled pattern of spilt petroleum, which completely covers it, motionless. A strip of dry, trampled meadow between the road along

the river and the water itself gently drops away, before
terminating in a steep paved embankment. Anglers crouch
there, bottoms resting on their heels, the soles of their feet
firmly attached to the precipitous stone. From the riverside
path, all one can see are the yellow fishing rods swaying
back and forth, their ends twitching, before they freeze. A
man – accablé! – sits motionless, crushed by bold glaring light,
midstream in a shallow boat, which has been hitched to two
poles, small, dark and scrawny, with his knees pulled up. On
the other bank, the long river island is covered in a jungle
of tall scrubby meadows with dank, grim shadows beneath.
Sunken barge, half overturned. Silvery-grey wood, concrete?
A breath of wind seems to brush past occasionally, the odd
tree starting to breathe in the silvery air [blank], but it does
not make it across the water. Some protruding branches are
completely stripped bare. Beyond, lifeless factory chimneys,
tiled roofs and, slowly rising up under its heavy mantle of
round grey trees in the parks, Mont Valérien, covered by low
straggling barrack buildings. On its flank, smothered by tree-
tops and stone walls, or perhaps further back, in the woods,
under the oppressive shadow of cloud, the occasional dry
crack of cannon fire. And the ubiquitous aeroplane, invisibly
hunting around, boring away like an angry, flat-headed wasp.

The city nearby has emptied human shapes onto the strip
of meadow by the river; they lie shrunken, hardly breathing, their stomachs flat, in thin anaemic sleep. Girls beside
bicycles on their sides, their skinny hips sticking up abruptly,
while their head and shoulders are blurred by the grass. A
little man laid out as stiff as a poker, his flat straw hat over

his face. A child, upper body propped up on a skinny arm, her head almost nothing but drab light-brown hair, dead straight, collapsing onto her shoulders. The little dirty face, dark nostrils, the eyes half-concealed by hair. [blank] She wears a checked smock, a broad pinafore dress, drawn in at the waist by a length of material which has been wound round and round. The sleeping young man has made a workmanlike job of blocking himself off from the outside world, his slender hands tucked behind his neck, bare ankles delicately crossed. The once decent black jacket is too short, with holes under the arms, the cracked toes of his shallow yellow shoes gleaming like old ivory.

A motorboat, its bow protruding, the single great bow wave washing right up the embankment. The stiff fluttering flag, in the still air, exerts a peculiar effect. The angler clutches hold of the pole, his boat writhing. Sailors at the controls, one with a casual hand on the steering wheel, officers in the stern, white jackets, hands tucked into their fronts; one glances at his watch.

Courtyard of the Hôtel Sully
Rue Saint-Honoré

The vaulted interior of the gateway is a mass of stuccoed coffering. No porter's lodge, an enclosed damp wall on either side, a collection of dustbins. The vault sends you, speechless,

straight in among all the heavy surmounted windows in
the courtyard. The skinny black cat with sleek wavy fur
wearing a tight collar with a bell. It presses its stomach to
the ground if you reach for it, stretching out with its head
thrown back, the tail continuing to trace slow, absent-minded
circles. Rough cobbles; how the cannon must have roared.
Golden-green moss grows in the pointing, with grass towards
the ground and pale-green weeds in the damp corners. An
unbalanced draw well, strangely austere for an enormously
wealthy hôtel, squeezed to one side of the barren cobbles,
a rusty wheel above a low cylinder of stone. In front of the
doorway to the corps de logis, a terrace of two shallow steps
juts out, extending across the whole width of the courtyard.
Half-submerged guard stones the colour of bone form a thin
row in front. The two sphinxes, mounted on low plinths
parallel to the main building, appear to have been made
from the same stone. Painfully, with almost no necks, they
raise their heads to the vertical. A Fury's long cascading hair
and enormous sagging breasts awkwardly disguise the tran-
sition into the lion's body. They are gaunt, jaded, their ribs
protruding. The tail with its impressive tuft lies neatly placed
across the rump, continuing along the belly. Their backs are
never scorched by the sun: the square well of the courtyard
is dark and cramped; the bluey-purple sky, shot through
with gold, seems impossibly high. Only the lucarnes with
the heavy flattened curve of their pediments and the steep
slate mansard roofs are still streaked with light, but it lies
strangely transmuted upon them, like fine golden lichen. The
bonnets on the dormer windows protrude out of the façade

like battlements, only broken up by the cornicing and the lead-grey gutters. [blank] Half a geranium cluster, a couple of tiny red coloured tiles, quite close to and warm [blank]. They are only visible if one looks directly at them, like a minor star at daybreak. The roof with its thousands of slate tiles, each reacting differently to the light. Some are rough, dull, absorbing it; others gleam like glass. Brownish ones, purple. – The windows all have the same segmented pediment, featuring a woman's head and a set of antlers of sorts. Heavy garlands of fruit beneath. No shutters. Everywhere only that blackish stone. Some windows smeared with a milky blue; others half-veiled by blinds made from matting. Above the compressed, choked central doorway, two long, narrow niches, which extend over two floors. In them are statues, endeavouring to reach the top while also keeping their massive limbs within the confined space. A stocky old man, his robes hitched up, a club jammed under his arm. Gnarled, bald head. A youth, bunches of grapes in both hands, one pressed to his neck, the other against his hip. The communs* have identical niches in the same place, into which enormous female figures have been confined. One can only see their massive thighs and breasts, the elbows poking out of the façade. To the right, on the ground floor, garages have been erected behind rough gates encrusted with yellowy-brown paint, into which a round hole has been cut to serve as a window. Next to it is the concierge's door. A wicker stool, like one from a church, with a ball of wool

---

*   Side buildings.

on it. The rustle of a newspaper, the sizzle of a frying pan. The smell does not carry.

Blackout

The sparse lamps, with their long black card sleeves, cast [blank] at the carrefours, dull flashes being picked up by panes of glass, gold lettering on shops, the golden animal heads on the boucheries, cafés. Most of the shops behind heavy lead-grey curtains of sheet metal. The blackout cloth on the café's revolving door, too short, in constant motion, light swashing out. On the empty terrace, in the first row of tables, a sleeping clochard, his bags on the chairs alongside. His head is sunk forward, into the gaping neck of his coat. The purr of dynamos, the lights on approaching bicycles sweeping from one side of the street to the other, long winking beams which, when they pass under a streetlight, become small, myopic, wall-eyed. Strings of tiny blue lights bar the way, denoting torn-up cobblestones. Running aground into banks of sand. A squaddie, running late, scurries along the middle of the street, a jangle of metal always coming a fraction of a second after the thud of his boot. The silence of those dodging him. The cat in the gutter, like a patch of the darkest damp: it recoils, padding across the street. The face of someone which does not light up when they brush past, revealing only a bluish sheen, followed by the muted white of two large eyeballs: a negro. The tall, arched gates, panelled and studded, are closed. But the narrow door cut into them is unlocked, yielding when one pushes against it, noiselessly, into the deep black of the gateway. It does not quite reach the ground; one must lift one's legs over the remaining strip of gate, like in bulkheads on a ship. Out of one, the slippered feet of a concierge emerge, the [blank] Out of another, one after the other, come three male figures [blank] Lean, in loose-fitting black suits, they appear to be carrying heavy bags.

The gardens leading up to the Terrasse at Saint-Germain

The steep, short break in the undulating woodland of the Seine valley. A lush overgrown ridge. The river has pushed itself away, with a flat strip of alluvial soil. Orchards, for the most part neglected, narrow vineyards (one cannot see any grapes), kitchen gardens. Pale green lettuces, the jungle of beanstalks, cabbages in short rows, kohlrabi tubers, heavy nodding poppy heads. Some swamped by thick weeds, the shape of the plants blurred, the only indication individual cabbages which have bolted. Untended since the year before, the gardens hold their ground spontaneously against the jungle of weeds, through self-seeding. Slumped scarecrows, bags stuffed with straw. Large yellowy-blue squashes balancing gingerly on the dry topsoil. Other plots completely consumed by dense forests of shrubs; clematis woven into a solid mass. In certain places, it is still flowering with thousands of yellow-white dots and stars; in others, with its feathery seed heads, it forms a grey cloud, spanning the space between the trees in soft [blank], weaving up towards the top. Elsewhere it is dead woody strands which shackle the trunks, pulling them down. Alders form the bulk. One can make out a solitary old cherry tree with its dull leaves, already brown in places. The unshakeably pure, clearly defined shape of the sycamore. The overripe reddish-blue clusters of elderberries. Huge stinging nettles and burdocks mingle from below, the hairs on their uppermost leaves tinged red.

Towards the octagon at the northern end of the Terrasse the ground is less steep, approaching from some way away and reaching higher up. In tall thin grass stand hundreds of stunted fruit trees. The soil here must be particularly poor. Swallows dart overhead, flying low, criss-crossing with frenzied little cries. In one tree one comes across – the mouth puckering, athirst, with sharpness – colonies of little reddish-green apples. – Overcast sky, south-west wind, localized rain; afternoon. Clouds coming across from the Marly aqueduct.

The fierce, yet short-winded attempt by the vegetation on the river plain to surge up towards the elongated Terrasse, tying itself in knots.

Boulevard Montmartre

In the west, at street level, the sky still glows (one cannot look at it), slowly cooling via yellow, green, purple. Long, solid, green rays through the tops of the plane trees. Alpenglow on some of the roofs along one side of the street. A delicate pink, of which soon only a purplish-white fluorescence remains. Up on the last, the highest of the narrow balconies, are women in peignoirs; gaunt, hollow cheeks. Two stand with their arms around each other's waists. It soon gets dark. The sky turns lilac, greyish-blue. The scattered clouds, ablaze a moment ago, are nothing but blotches, expanses of dark brown. Looking between the motionless walls of plane trees, one can see a section of recessed balcony on one façade, painted a reddish brown. Lifeless illuminated letters. Men in shirtsleeves lounge in the windows. A café – red and blue neon lights – being swept out by the garçon, his apron hanging down almost to the ground. Another, unfashionably déserté, with heavy imitation wood panelling and a coffered ceiling; four laid tables, only one with a customer. – – Music, of varying richness – excited twittering behind fabric, glass – trumpet blasts blaring out onto the street. German marches, "Das kann doch einen Seemann nicht erschüttern".* All-female dance bands mostly, the first violinist nubile, slim, with horn-rimmed spectacles and a high forehead.

---

* A song from the 1939 comedy film *Paradies der Junggesellen* (*Bachelors' Paradise*).

Only the back row of tables on the café terrace is occupied. Bourgeois couples in silence, looking in opposite directions. Only a few passers-by; their eyes follow them for a time.
Man in a beret, grey side-whiskers, Légion d'honneur rosette.
Bière Koenigshofen, Tiger beer. Single ladies, unsettled parce
que "l'entrée au café est interdite aux dames seules". One
can see their outline against the light from inside: the strong,
agile chin, the little straw hat which has slipped forward,
askew. Summer furs, good for fluffing up.

The flow of people outside continues to swell, often
backing up outside the entrance to the café, in the narrow
inlet between the tables. Especially if the band is playing.
Clochards with slanting shoulders, open mouths, forearms
buried in endless bags. One scratches his beard, deep in
thought. The waiter comes slowly over, without looking at
him, closer; the clochard straightens his sack and puts out
to sea once more. "Professeurs" with broad slouching hats,
thick bamboo walking sticks, oversized gaiters and wrinkled
faces lemon yellow or the colour of parchment. Garde mobile
in pairs, well-fed coppery faces, thumbs in their shoulder
straps, sauntering along, in lively conversation. An imbecile
with watery eyes and cropped, fuzzy hair, his buttoned-up
green coat seemingly his only item of clothing. A tall negro
gentleman in a snappy blue suit, pale felt shoes, carrying a
heavy walking stick.

It gets darker and darker and the worm of people begins
to sprawl more and more. The scraping, clattering of thousands of shoes, sandals, soldiers' hooves. The number of soldiers now increasing by the minute. Whole bunches around

the non-coms, stumbling on, faltering; stragglers' eyes are caught by the girls, before they come lumbering up behind. Into a bar, and then the next minute spat back out onto the street: there was nothing going on. Loners, small and mean; older territorials, long breeches flapping down over lace-up boots with domed, distended toecaps. A bayonet dangling somewhere by a skinny behind, shoulders sloping sharply. A moustache the width of your thumb, a gold tooth; beneath the tan an anaemic, measly face. They stand for hours by shop windows, their arms behind their backs, before shambling across the street towards a girl. There's a very casual approach to saluting; the night swallows up the silver braid, and one can hardly raise one's arm in the throng. The officers don't set much store by it, either; they seem in a hurry, irritated by the delay, and, blinking, try to turn round but briefly. A little lieutenant, with scrubbed, chubby cheeks, races past several times, for completely no reason, brushing the terrace like a lawnmower. A conscript, pale, slight, with horn-rimmed spectacles, is the first to take a seat at the front row of tables; uneasy on his chair, he twists his neck, then gets up, without having had a drink. OT men,[*] speaking in a dreadful mush of dialects, and always at the tops of their voices. Narrow-brimmed Tyrolean hats, breeches, leather coats.

And, along with the soldiers, a real mass of girls. Always the same type, repeated a hundredfold: the non-professionals. Small, stocky, bareheaded, the glossy, dark black hair that

---

[*] Set up by the Nazis in 1933, the Organisation Todt ('OT') was responsible for engineering projects.

should be left to grow scraped right back, one frisette across the shoulders, another across the forehead, always the same shape. Bare legs, high-heeled sandals, clacking wooden soles. A suit jacket hanging across the shoulders, a twirling little handbag. In twos, fours, laughing with their heads together, whispering. Très sportives. They are onto the squaddies in a flash, and know various bits of German: no gud – no expensive – leesten – gud bye etc. Their conversation draws uninhibited looks from any of their fellow countrymen strolling by. They lock step with the squaddies, hooking their arms through theirs, or wrapping them around them. Two girls, one of them wearing a thin coat of fake panther skin. First, they negotiate with two stolid, senior flak lance corporals in a doorway, then they tramp past on their own, then back again with two slouching little infantrymen. Opposite are the real "poules", a significant minority group. In their big hats, high heels, furs weighing on their shoulders, they look like tall stately caravels among the common fishing smacks. Complete disregard for the other prevails between the two groups. But the classic [blank] the way they imperceptibly slow down, showing their figures to advantage, look behind them, then come back, is somehow wasted. It is rare to see one who has managed to draw a little squaddie, like a schoolboy, to one side, coaxing him with slow, deliberate words. He shakes his head, counting out with his fingers. Domestic trade seems to be entirely out of the question; one can see a hunger in the flâneurs' eyes, but their faces remain switched off, unassuaged. – Wreaths of straw come slowly floating across, newsgirls with their dry lifeless blond hair. They have taken off their caps, studying them with affection, abandoned. Unhurriedly leading from the hip, as if the flow bore them in its midst when, in actual fact, each wave avoids them. Even German civilians survive being swallowed up, going under, bobbing along like blown-up pigs' bladders. Yesterday's overindulgences, still not fully digested, in no way dampen the restless, greedy and yet dismissive looks on their faces: taking it all in, not missing a thing, but never attracting attention; not getting caught where it doesn't pay to or where they aren't allowed. There aren't any good seats left here; that tart's legs are too thin; the café opposite looks like a swizz. The waiter straightens a table, the girl takes her handbag from a neighbouring chair – but of the Allemand one can only see the folds of his neck. An insincere sweet-and-sour smile hoisted across the lips or the blatant jutting chin of a criminal. Some strut along with a ponderous rocking motion, others are hunched: they seem keen to sneak away in their mackintoshes, self-effacing, as if they did not exist. – An attractive, almost provocatively dressed boy stands motionless by one of the tables, earnestly trying to catch the punters' eyes. Silken jet-black hair, a great whorl at the back of his head, his fringe coming down almost to his eyebrows. On being asked by the waiter why he is not in bed: "Mais, j'ai douze ans, je porte une cravate." And the old woman with the great green woollen shawl who stands for hours, as if turned to stone, in the dark shadows beside the newspaper kiosk, her bare arms folded across her chest. The kiosk itself has become a dazzling beacon of light; it streams from the window, from underneath, moulding the forehead of the woman who runs it into thick bulges. – Now one can discern solid middle-class couples, gens très bien, who have eaten together in the restaurant, [one word illegible] saying goodbye to each other. Trim ladies in immaculate tailored suits, hair swept up from the neck, a tightly furled umbrella hanging from their arm.

They all glide past each other, only inches apart, and yet stay separate, without getting mixed up. Each and every *Blitzmädchen*, primed to clock a particular occurrence in a matter of seconds in the last corner of the twilit [blank], without the possibility of being drawn as a witness, evading a scuffle, a patrol, disappearing into the Métro.

The leaves of the plane trees, houses, and the sky now form one great dark mass. In the west [blank], and only there, incombustible in the icy luminous ether, the first trembling stars appear. The street is already emptying as the shadow of curfew approaches. The few solitary customers on the café terrace feel their scarcity value increasing by the minute. The girls increasingly parade into the inlets, for longer and longer [blank] Wherever they look, they encounter the same broad white faces, the gleaming [blank] eyes. The violin cases snap shut; somewhere chairs are being stacked. The waiters in one lonely corner, as yet unconsumed by the icy glow. It becomes thinner, hollower, just a narrow glacial strip beyond the black chimneys. But there is a constant, even whiter light, a frosted green. What, with each passing second, is lost in intensity, is revealed in the first stars which suddenly appear beyond, trembling. They initially seem to congeal, to suffocate. But then they can breathe comfortably again, swelling evenly in tone. The darkness has become too thick, above the trees and the rooftops. The street is empty now, the approaching curfew sucking out the Métro stations, the furthermost boulevards, where the barracks lie. The café regulars have gone, after a brief friendly exchange with the garçon – Que voulez-vous... il faut se débrouiller... on vit de jour en jour – waddling across the street towards that gap between the conveniences and the newspaper kiosk, the sweaty dark passage; they live close by. At the back of the café, violin cases snap shut, strings of bulbs are extinguished, the darkness slumping down after an inexplicable moment's pause. The girls increasingly position themselves, for longer and longer, at the inlets, channels on the terrace. The few solitary customers feel their scarcity value increasing by the minute. Wherever they look, they encounter the same broad white faces, the gleaming eyes which slowly elude, then are suddenly back, the dark mouths drooping, on the verge of a nervous smile. The waiter empties his pockets onto a far table, picking through the coins with holes in the middle.* The window right at the top which has not been covered up. Flapping curtains. A scraggy, naked figure disrupts a yellow-orange light: it shines out around his arms, between his legs. An enormous shadow joins in on the opposite side of the street. Beneath the roots of the trees, the roar of the last Métro.

---

* i.e. Occupation Reichsmark coins.

The bastion

The long corridors, parallel to the station concourse, with, for long stretches along the left, frosted glass windows onto the station, offering little light; on the right, bedroom doors, in their hundreds. Although there is a constant draught, the air is always musty. It smells of rancid fat; others believe it to be dead mice. Outside the room belonging to Fräulein X., secretary to the head of the embassy's vehicle fleet, there is a definite whiff of the zoo: the lady keeps a parrot, white mice, and offers board and lodging to various dogs. – Endless carpets running down the corridors. In some places there are electric lights on even during the day. A passageway branches off, in which there stand battered brass bedsteads. Fire buckets with cigarette stubs at regular intervals. The "*office*": normally no one is in. The room service waiters – 2½ men for almost 500 rooms – are constantly on the go. Hot, a gas hob burning, a tap dripping onto zinc. After calling for a while, a pot washer appears, unshaven, sleeves rolled up. Bustling women sometimes pop in to get themselves a plate, a knife.

The hotel, which has seen better days, was built as part of the station. The Orléans–Bordeaux line. In the past, there would have been people coming in from the provinces, wholesale merchants from Bordeaux, faux ménages (there are two exits). Receptions, meetings in the great dining room which is now used for permit checks. And, at one time, outstanding cuisine. Mauriac often used to get off here and encounter genuine Bordelais characters from his novels. Claudel: très distant, plutôt rébarbatif according to the chef de réception. Maurois, who lived nearby, in the Rue de Poitiers, rented a little room on the fifth floor, to which he often withdrew.

Morning. Ladies' shoes, tight military boots which bend at the ankle. All manner of combinations. Down the corridor, a pale triangle drops out of an open bedroom door onto the carpet; the back of a femme de chambre, with crossed white apron straps, appears, brooms propped up outside: an early riser's room being made up straight away. The shoes only start to disappear from half past eight. Whooshing bathwater, sometimes accompanied by a gramophone. Frightful acoustics in the tiled salles de bains. On the fifth floor, where looser morals prevail (or rather: there's all kinds going on), one encounters single ladies in arresting peignoirs on the way to the bathroom. (There are lots of little rooms to be found there, most of them without facilities. There is no roof structure above; très chaud en été. Broad, balcony-like eaves beneath the dormer windows. Leaning out, to the left one can just see Notre-Dame, followed by the Panthéon and Val-de-Grâce, the grey skeleton of the unfinished block in the Rue Jacob; to the right, the Dôme des Invalides, and the two stocky skewers of Sainte-Clothilde etc.) Room service staff scoot across the carpets: a hive of activity, as nearly all the milords and ladies breakfast in bed. The heavy tray clamped at shoulder height, head tucked at an angle. The other hand is for opening doors. The long coat-tails like the wing-cases of giant beetles. One, with thick horn-rimmed spectacles, sweaty red face, a strong smell of wine sometimes trailing behind him, is a farmer's boy from Picardy. The stiff curved shirt front, clippers for ration cards in his pocket on a silver chain. Always out of puff, limited options with those great red hands. The tray only just fits through the door. Larger meals are brought on a table – no wheels, but the feet are fitted with shiny discs – carried and lifted using only the elbows, even up stairs. Then pushed into the rooms, gliding casily across the carpet. If they are in a hurry and break into a trot, the air parts with an audible swoosh. A squaddie clatters out of one door, stealing a glance down the corridor before taking the service stairs. Silently, from another, a final plume of smoke swirling in the room behind him, slips a diplomat, or at least somebody wearing a diplomat's uniform, rosy-cheeked, impeccably shaven and splashed with scent. Tellingly, he answers the Nazi salute after a second's hesitation and with a somewhat plaintive sluggishness. ("Who's that chap – can't remember – there's no way anyone can remember all these faces.") He jogs a couple of paces while looking at his wristwatch before lapsing back into the easy swaying gait of the attaché, his steps only a trifle overdone. He gravely returns the salute to a squaddie he passes, but with a certain remoteness. (Allegedly put himself forward several times in the past but, as you know, no one gets out of here.) – The dumpy little "gouvernante", the terror of the valets. A fearsome bark, in good French, aquiline nose, sensible hairstyle, delicate make-up. She wears severe, dark suits, sometimes with a tie. She will only exchange short, measured greetings with a couple of Allemands; on some she will bestow a little apologetic smile – senior embassy men mainly, who date from "avant". As far she is concerned, all the rest of the personnel – staff, agents of various types, flics, the typing pool, chauffeurs, orderlies etc. – do not exist.

The rooms are yellow-gold and blue. The bergères covered with faded blue velvet(?), the table thin-legged and narrow, a real lack of drawers, bahuts etc. The bed enormous, almost square, the dark blue eiderdown (quilt?), initially very tired and thin, then swapped for a new one, with a metallic sheen. Every room has the same white marble fireplace which has never been used and has been sealed up with an iron shutter. On it, an electric clock and two very delicate candelabra (minus candles), tinted red-gold. In the evening, the femme de chambre knocks. In answer to the grumpy "Entrez!", she twitters in alarm: "Oh – excusez-moi – c'était pour fermer les persiennes…" A mumbled reply… "Bien – je – fermé – moi même." Then, from outside, the coda: "Alors, excusez-moi, bonsoir, monsieur." – The hotel staff's laxity in following blackout regulations is the cause of frequent warnings from the city commandant or the Sûreté; endlessly reproduced reminders adorn the lifts, trays etc., or are tucked under the glass tops of the tables.

The walls are thin. No doubt about that. The headboard of the bed lies under the telephone of the neighbouring room: "Hello. How are you?… Where do you want to meet, then?… Where? Never heard of it… Where we were the day before yesterday. OK, fine.… Oh, you know I'm bringing someone… We can talk about that then… I'll call round to see them afterwards…"

The two young men frequently eat together of an evening in the room. A *souper* ordered from the *office*, bolstered by privately sourced victuals. "Tin of sardines – artificial honey – straight from the source. That shop in the little street off the Boulevard Saint-Germain... It's for embassy staff only... but don't spread it around... It's the woman I got the pass for. Husband's in prison in Germany. Officer in the air force... You can swap bread stamps for suit cloth, as much as you like... This wine's corked. That can go straight back. Pass me the phone. The waiter's having a laugh... Best thing is to call réception... And don't stand for any nonsense..."

Their successor – the two friends' departure was rather sudden, following a lengthy visit by a gentleman in a brown shirt, blue suit, black leather coat – has a strong southern accent; anyway, she speaks fluent French on the telephone, and makes things difficult for the femme de chambre. Sometimes she hooks up with a squaddie with a deep bass voice, which she endeavours to suppress with constant shushing. "Bloody hell, haven't you got a bootjack?... And don't you shush me. I've had enough of your squealing..." – "Hey, that's a bit saucy... comme çi... comme ça... ooh-la-la..." Fortunately, just then a train pulls into the station below. The whole hotel, candelabra, trays and windows vibrate for several minutes. All one can hear from the neighbouring room is a post-coital quiet. Until the squaddie's unnaturally loud pronouncement: "Ee, I could pee like a racehorse." "What a delightful turn of phrase you have." "When d'you wanna meet up again?" "Don't know. Not tomorrow... I'll call you... Oh, and make sure no one sees you when you leave... I'm sure to lose my position otherwise."

At night, sometimes difficulties with a key arise outside the door of a neighbouring room. Protracted jabbing at the lock, suppressed swearing. Finally, they find the keyhole and go in; immediately followed by the whoosh of the bath, at two in the morning. Piercing whistle blasts from the street: "Lumière troisième!" More police whistles. Finally, the persiennes squeak, the curtains swish. The returnee has got it: blackout. Shoes are flung into a corner, and then the deep, groaning slump into bed. He repeats the new phrase he had learnt tonight, revelling in each syllable: "Grande – poule – de – luxe." Lights out. – Sometimes there's a bash nearby. Lucienne Boyer singing "Parlez-moi..." or "Temps des cerises" from a gramophone packed round with pillows. Bottles of champagne are given a good dousing in the bathroom. Particularly hospitable are a lecturer and his young wife, who, as advertised in the lift, teaches "Gymnastics for German women." Night-time calls are popular, to people who have not been invited, both acquaintances and complete strangers. "Is that Fräulein Meyer?" "Who? What? This is X., secretary to the legation. There should be... Intolerable, waking a man up in the middle of the night. I shall have the police clear your room. No, wait: I shall speak to the ambassador tomorrow... I'm sure you'd enjoy being back in the ranks. You'll be hearing from me again!... Heil Hitler!"

The old professor in his cramped room between the lift and the loo. His cases stand outside in the corridor, a neat tower. Piles of old newspapers (he throws nothing away) he hasn't got around to reading. A run of Baedekers, in two, three copies. A gnarled walking stick with an iron tip, for the summer a large yellowy-white panama hat, a lemon-yellow linen-silk jacket. Cognac bottles on the mantelpiece. Several deluxe editions of "Fleurs du mal" with nude lithographs one can take out. "Nuits arabes", "Jardin des supplices" etc. He has discovered a bookshop on Place (Rue?) Furstenberg where, on certain days, there is better pornography to be had. Electric stove with never-ending lengths of flex, various old meal trays missing from the *office*. Books in his coat pockets, trousers billowing like Aeolus. Often on the telephone speaking to "colleagues", who are not. The femme de chambre must get a shock when she enters the room. Quelle odeur! Even the little tailor who is constantly being forced on him has to make an effort to maintain his composure.

The lift. Three operators. The tall, lean Indian, a wiry, leathery marionette, the picture of politeness and jollity. The diminutive, buzzing little Celt with the narrow moustache, swept-up hair and an amiable grimacing little mug. He only smelt of drink the once, leaning against the side of the lift, late at night; he had to spend hours ferrying air force officers up and down, when there was a Luftwaffe ball on the first floor. "Ça donne dans les jambes – il y a du monde ce soir – ooh-la-la." The adolescent chasseur who helps out, never raising his eyes from his little paperback crime novel, operating the lift buttons without looking up. His face abloom with thousands of purple pimples.

The nice loo attendant in the narrow passageway between the hotel foyer and the waiting-room restaurant. She is always dressed in a smock of forget-me-not blue and has the gentlest, deepest, most obliging of voices. Dark hair cut short, the fringe hanging down low over her forehead, the back of the head heavier, with a snappy hairline. Is she a Slav? Polish? The large, somewhat bulbous nose, even the chin is large and long, the cheeks broad and slightly concave. The telephone cubicle is also part of her domain, a terrific soundbox. Speakers constantly try to pull the door to from inside; it doesn't latch. Naïve vainqueurs telephone the outside world from here: "Est-ce que je pourrai parler avec Mademoiselle Yvette?... Comment? Yvette quoi? Mais je sais seulement qu'elle s'appelle Yvette... Elle n'est pas là?... Mais elle m'avait dit... Quoi? Je ne peux pas comprendre..." etc.

The waiting-room restaurant and its fauna. A large, chaotic, draughty room, heavy stuccoed ceiling; a jumble of all manner of glaring lights, which burn even by day. Glass walls and folding screens, with sofas positioned back-to-back, in a vain attempt to break up the room. Somewhere there is a dividing line between the area set aside "pour l'ambassade allemande" and the portion designated for waiting-room customers – largely better types from the quiet streets of the Quartier Saint-Germain who turn up day after day. In the centre, in the shade of a potted palm, a structure with baskets of fruit and a soup tureen over a gas burner, sometimes with even the odd crayfish or lobster on offer. That is where Suzanne waits, a bustling little trainee, bow-legged but otherwise shapely, drawing eyes from all around the room. Cursory absent-minded glances which, much as they try not to, keep drifting back to her, leaving other faces convulsed with resentment. Or the artifice of relentless furtive glances, entirely focused, but which nevertheless do not stop the gentleman concerned from being sullen when ordering or keeping tabs on his *tickets*. For Suzanne's primary duty is clipping ration cards, for which the more learned diners dub her with names such as Atropos, la Guerrière, l'Inexorable etc. Suzanne takes no notice of these and, without catching anyone's eye, and avoiding chance contact, glides between the legs of both chairs and men. Her scissors twitter. She has long been held in high esteem by Professor X. as sprightly, vivacious, housewifely etc. He looks, with a gentle smile, down the top of her tunic, his hand in his pocket, as she cuts his card. But once, when she cut off three times the requisite number of squares for his meat ration, he could contain himself no longer. He took his hand from his pocket and uttered the following not entirely comprehensible double clause: "Vous me connaissez, et vous me connaitrez…!" – "Elle a déjà eu des petits," the waiter informed him. "Mais, vous savez, supprimés." Then Suzanne actually does get married, to a boxer, de Montmartre. One of her German admirers is keen to see him: an ugly debauched creature. The honeymoon lasts exactly three days. As the hot summer months approach, Suzanne shows increasing signs of advanced pregnancy. No more joshing and japing with the garçons (she was also a past master at tripping people up); she sometimes leans, pale-faced, over her silver soup tureen, her hands in the pockets of her white tunic. Her hair no longer looks quite right, her forehead seems angular, squashed, the bold nose too short, anaemic. – It is also where the "sommelier" usually hangs around, rather bleary-eyed, heavyset, with wonderful burgundy-coloured cheeks and a grey handlebar moustache. Today the last "Pelure d'Oignon" went, to two German airmen to whom one could just as well have served tomato juice. With a noble stoop, drooping ends to his moustache and the golden dust of the cellar to his voice, he receives the Boches' sacrilegious orders for beer and seltzer water, and their preposterous complaints.

Packages tucked under their arms, collars turned up, cooks and pot washers squeeze past through here when it is time to go home; bent, haggard figures. Every evening, on a long table by the wall, there are several hundred lunch bags, a half-bottle of red wine poking out of each. "C'est pour les juifs qui partent pour le Brésil," wonders a garçon. They are then loaded onto a van on the station platform used for transporting luggage which, with a great rumble and a clatter, manoeuvres its way through the swing doors.

The old German admiral with the incredibly large, weathered nose and narrow, grey, lashless eyes. When he reads the despatches from Italy, he puffs out his cheeks. Revered by the staff, surrounded by folding screens. He is here on behalf of the Zeughaus* in Berlin. His man/assistant, an arrogant know-it-all student in a lance corporal's uniform.

The Ogou [i.e. Hautgoût?] corner, noisy as a fish shop. Sofas with a wide view. The tubby little man with a rigid artificial hand, in a glove. With no real back to his head, and

---

* The old Prussian arsenal building on Unter den Linden, from the late nineteenth century onwards a military museum.

no neck, the face poorly set and stitched together somewhere. Keen on meeting everyone, shaking everybody's hand, constantly popping up behind the table. A tall thin corporal with steel-rimmed spectacles, with likewise no back to his head, but furnished with angular jug ears; an alarming lack of chin, which seems to have been swallowed, only to consolidate with his Adam's apple. His face is pale and measly; his neighbour's, in contrast, well nourished and ruddy. But he is constantly prying around the room with his overly bright eyes. Les requins.

Journalists, press attachés, propaganda squadron, Rosenberg Taskforce*: nothing but pretty little things, us! Only a couple of minor flaws: the tie a little too light, the hair too thin, a neck too full, an ear overworked. Rather too many nervous hand gestures: two ring-covered fingers up by the temples, pushing the skin into a couple of folds; a forefinger and thumb picking something off a chin, out of the dimple. They've seen ugliness, of course. Captured during the German invasion of Brussels, sent off to France in sealed trains, standing up for days on end with nothing to drink and given a miserable thrashing by the Sûreté. Things are bearable now, certainly. But for how long? S. has been detailed to Warsaw and R., who had that bother over the figures, was called up overnight.

They help themselves while filing to [blank] Then they run their hand through their scented hair, shoot their cuffs.

---

* A Nazi organization tasked with appropriating cultural property during the war.

A quick, searching glance around the room: a slight bow and a click of heels, a raised arm, and you're given a table in some far-flung corner. Conversations with the waiter are long and low. Not very far with the French yet, but that doesn't really matter. A confident manner and knowing your way around a menu are much more important. "Can I offer you a Corton?... Or perhaps a Chablis today?... Is the rôti passable?... It's now official: apparently Roosevelt is Jewish... Did you read about that English aircraft carrier? Amazing... Wasn't that a great place yesterday? Just Luftwaffe and French there... Nice birds... That nineteen-year-old Creole girl... wonderful hip action... Do you know Baudelaire?... Have you seen Andrée, no, what's she called, in Baty's play?... Very interesting, but the French can't do Shakespeare. Too precious... didn't work... I need a couple of dates from you for the diary..."

The sequestered ministry

The railings: a row of gold-tipped lances, head-height on a plinth wall. Lilac bushes beyond. The front room of the little one-storey lodge building serves as the guardroom and accommodates a half-dozen young airmen. A great fire crackles in the grate, accompanied by reflections, from antique gold and the legs of gleaming boots. A radio pours from the windowsill, but there is a piano going, too: the pianist, hollow back, belt and webbing, attempting to reconstruct a popular song he heard yesterday in Montmartre. Beside him a messmate, lost in reverie, his milk-white cheek propped in his hand, occasionally hitting one of the lower notes with the stem of his pipe; in answer, a heart-rending yawn from the back room. Everything is swathed in blue smoke. The furnishings, some badly damaged, consist of a variety of sumptuous armchairs and couches, which cannot conceal their origins in the ministry salons. On the mantelpiece, a magnificent pendule in a case made of pink marble or porphyry with ormolu fittings. Beside it: army helmets, tinned meat. Engloûti. In the depths of one of these armchairs, a man with a knitted brow reads a "True Stories" magazine. Initially, he does not react to the corporal's shout, as if the frequency were simply not on his radar. The corporal is filling in the guard book. Swaying next to him, one of the charwomen from the Palais, large, voluptuous, middle-aged; she coughs into her thin fur stole: "On étouffe avec cette fumée" and attempts, in vain, to sell him a bar of cooking chocolate. When she taps on his shoulder, he treats her to a friendly poke in the stomach: "Will you sod off... bitch." – After a general stuck his oar in, some of the fauteuils are retired and a gun rack constructed. – Outside stands a wheelbarrow full of chopped-up, freshly sawn branches, as thick as your arm; the ministry garden is like a park. In the summer, a couple of the ostentatious seating options are pushed outside. Right next to the wall there is an area, hidden from the street: the perfect spot for sitting in the sun. Squashed down across the chair, legs hooked over the armrests, arms folded behind one's head. Comfortable it is not, but one should not be fazed by opulent furniture. The tight blue knees, the creases still just discernible, higher than one's head and splayed apart, distant peaks in the hot shimmering air. A cloud of sparrows blustering in the faded lilac bushes – the golden lances aquiver and the gravel soon baked hard in the heat…

Half a seal still clings to the door of the long Archive wing. Midday and the stairwell still plunged in darkness. On the third floor, one of the initial rooms serves as the control room for the secret military police, the GFP. A pervading smell of Harz Mountain cheese and Fougère royale. The men, in slippers and cardigans, polish off slices of bread and butter. Parent unit: Fürth. A bright sea-green glow from the fireplace – the colour used to cover the Archive's tens of thousands of file boxes. On the mantelpiece, a row of plaster Columbines, in unsparingly short skirts, a collection of bronzes: charioteers, draped with sausage skins. A wonderful scene: Rafaelli? Hoarfrost, winter sun along the Quai des Tournelles, looking through the shimmering frosty air onto the chancel of Notre-Dame. Blue, purple, yellow-white. – The adjoining rooms are divided up into individual bedrooms, as can be seen from the nameplates: Rifleman Weigel, Private, Colonel. Sofas, on which the heads of department used to take their afternoon naps, heavy silk brocade curtains for blankets. Lieutenant S. set up camp using some file boxes on Siam, refusing to empty them; he enjoys reading the files himself, and has specific instructions from the SS office. One of his men assisted him in overcoming any language difficulties, an extraordinarily friendly and obliging seminarian who can play the piano and type, and speaks good French. Reputedly from Alsace. It's not much of a life with the Bavarians. The loo broken, the lift stuck: there's always something to keep him busy. The actual head of the detachment, a captain and quite an old campaigner ("faithful to the end, but what a temper..." (Z[itsche].)), is currently in a military hospital in Amiens. One night, speeding at 100 kilometres per hour, straight into a tree; driver dead on impact. Lieutenant S. took part in defeating the Pilsudski Guard and flushing them out of the trees like squirrels with his pistol, but generally he gets on splendidly with everybody. Except the guards next door, in the Reichsmarschall Palais... they drive him crazy. Those stupid oafs with their sub-machine guns – he now lets his men keep watch with hand grenades in their belts. He has had one corridor, which connects the Palais and the Archive buildings, simply bricked up; someone has written in pencil on the nice white plaster: This way to the Reichsmarschall. The door which leads out into the garden on the ground floor has been boarded up with heavy wooden planks.

Hundreds of rooms line the long corridors. Every door smashed open, every cupboard, every writing desk broken into. The drawers hang pathetically out of the grandiose bureaux d'acajou. Streams of letters have poured onto the floor; draughts leaf through photograph albums. The dust is already a quarter of an inch thick. The result is like Pompeii: all the calendars say 14/6/40. Newspapers consumed by the sun: des formations blindées ennemies ont réussi à s'infiltrer… Les combats continuent sur tout le front… Maps of the Aisne sector, the Weygand Line. In the bare, tube-like room belonging to the huissier, who was just finishing off the post (the valise for Madrid; the courier was due to leave that evening), there is a kettle, a tin of sardines. Top hats, little ladies' umbrellas lie strewn across the tables, a powder puff. A tartan travelling rug with straps… L'exode… A novel in every drawer. At certain windows, the awning has slipped down, so that the room is bathed in a yellowy-brown half-light. Rooms in which only the dreary brown of pine cupboards, the green of lampshades and document folders, prevail. The rooms for heads of departments equipped with the best period furniture or gleaming with ultramodern glass and nickel steel. The walls of one reception room are completely covered in pigskin leather, edged with thin strips of glass-topped cherry wood, a golden-brown velvet carpet. Then one day the leather – in sections of up to two square metres – had been neatly cut out, revealing rough timberwork beneath. The offending implement, a little ministerial penknife, still lies on the glazed windowsill. – On some desks, whole banks of telephones, of all different vintages, in most cases the mouthpiece and receiver separate. A map of Norway with the landing zones hatched in blue. Europe with the German–Russian demarcation line added very much by hand. Poincaré's bumpy head staring down at you, Barthou's barbe carrée. The walls of the office of the sous-directeur d'Afrique are hung with dancers from Marrakesh, the slender backs of black women gripping their shoulders – large, darkened, reddish-brown photographs. A group of holy men. The four gentlemen concerned engaged in all kinds of activities, with majestic little pot bellies, alongside colourfully embroidered court officials, flashing teeth in tails. – Bottle after bottle of red wine and copying ink. One cupboard contains hundreds of white bow ties and starched dickies. – The fifth floor, built on top, low bare rooms, the corridors surmounted by a glass roof; in summer, it is unbearably hot. This is the home of the press department. In the corridors, bleached and curled by the heat, lie all the provincial German newspapers from the first months of the war, stacked up in neatly knotted bundles. One can step out onto the roof of the transverse wing. Burnt offerings on the stripped altar to the summer sun. Scorched moss and lichen; the sheet zinc, in which the trap doors and hatches are clad, is red-hot. An abandoned anti-aircraft gun emplacement made from sandbags; flyers; the withered corpse of a cat. In all directions there stretch towering clouds with tumescent crests and craws, but all of them only attaining a certain height and a long way away, their feet obscured by the grey-blue, purple, powdery light. The sea of roofs shimmers and seethes, the Dôme des Invalides unbearably bright. A dull crack, absorbed by the hot walls: a coal-gas bus backfiring. A school party crossing the Esplanade des Invalides. – –

The desolate, looted rooms exert an irresistible pull on the various guard-duty detachments, but also on all kinds of occupying civilians. One comes across stockpiled objects which have particular commercial or sentimental value: paperweights, electric light bulbs, seal boxes for international treaties etc. Somebody stored them away at some point and then either forgot or did not come back for them; or he has been using them to fuel weeks of parcels home. Prowling around the suites of rooms sometimes results in unwelcome encounters, unexpected surprises. The squaddie who has fallen asleep at a magnificent mahogany writing desk while reading "I Was Hitler's Maid".* The lift comes gliding up out of the depths of the building at a terrific rate. In one room, a electrolier ablaze with dozens of light bulbs. Complete strangers from completely unknown departments trying out typewriters (there are still some there, but completely shot), browsing the bookshelves. The thick carpets mean one can sneak up without being heard. Every time, one is greeted by the delayed raising of the arm, in fright, the blood running cold or pulse racing, an exchange of short probing glances. – Clocks which suddenly strike; the charred remains of private letters floating up from a fireplace; dripping water echoing from somewhere. The building is unheated the whole winter, et presque tous les tuyaux ont éclaté. The car horns from the Esplanade outside sound strangely thin and distant. It is never an entirely pleasurable experience, picking and rummaging ("Histoire de fouiller, manie de chercher," as the pompier, who comes to check the fireplugs, describes the situation): there are the constant draughts down your back, and splinters from the doors which have been kicked in.

The stairs. Total darkness, the shallow wooden steps rotten in places from water ingress. An unrolled length

---

* Perhaps referring to the fictional memoir published in 1940 under the name of "Pauline Kohler", a piece of British propaganda which was translated into several languages.

of loo roll, woven through the railings, acts as Ariadne's thread. Another stairwell seems to have served, before the Occupation, as a paper depository. The stacks of premium paper stored there should last several centuries. Piles of forms, over head-height, for télégrammes à l'arrivée, au départ, minutes, dépêches, handouts from one minister to another. Couverts from slim billet-doux format through to a metre long, of varying colours and paper quality. Little ivory-coloured cards for ministerial *dîners*, with a delicately embossed state emblem. New Year's greetings with a pen-and-ink view of the Quai d'Orsay, a little ribbon in red, white and blue, signed by Bounel etc. etc. On the wall, three large paintings: one depicts water, smoke, blue sky and a cluster of stovepipe funnels. The French fleet at Kronstadt in 189–. The second, the Congress of Paris 1857. The men still wearing silk knee breeches, bright stockings; the Russian military with terrifically thick epaulettes. A lean, hunched, dark-skinned man in a fez sidling up to the gracious, moon-faced Walewski. Number three: huge blue windows, casting light onto a sea of bald pates and blotting pads: the Hague Conference. On the landing, a plaster bust of France herself in a Phrygian cap. The dust on the eyelids, lips, finger-thick.

It is hot in the library, as it sits directly over the heating. Warm air rises up out of circular vents covered by lattice grilles. The fusty smell of dust and warm paper. The bookcases alternate with busts, statuettes of French foreign ministers. The "commis" and the secretaries of state of the Ancien Régime are present in their entirety, as engravings. Smashed display cases, a couple of medals and coins still

inside; ancient portfolios, pen-holders, feathered tricorn
hats. The assassination of the plenipotentiaries at Rastatt.
Knackfuß's "Völker Europas, wahrt eure heiligsten Güter",
signed. Medals on the floor, snaking curls of film, sashes.
An old copy of Champaigne's portrait of Richelieu. One
can crawl through below to reach a corridor chock-full of
bound journals. The presses are to some extent still intact, the
books sweltering, squashed together behind fine wire mesh;
in other places, almost empty. Odd piles of anti-German
literature, diplomatic "colour books" etc. suggestive of
large-scale operations aborted.

Ground floor, contrôle des étrangers. The card catalogue,
a cabinet with huge drawers which run gently on silent roll-
ers. The rods, on which the cards were threaded, bald, gleaming nickel; only a couple of slips stuck to them. The men in
grey and black, with their convoys of trucks which rolled in
every 1–2 months, carted everything away. Most of the rooms
have already been completely stripped bare, leaving a thin
layer of trampled cardboard, flimsy carbon paper covered
in typescript and the imprints of dirty jackboots. "Le com-
missaire spécial d'Annemasse... division spéciale de police...
direction générale de la sûreté nationale etc. La nommée X,
employée de M. Thyssen à Monte Carlo, se montre paisi-
blement hitlérienne; elle se trouve en relations intimes avec
le chauffeur T..." "À propos du nommé Schneider Franz,
figurant sur la cinquième liste des éléments terroristes..."
Half a corridor is still stuffed full to the ceiling with green
file boxes. When the convoy returns, the soldiers form a
chain from this pile out to the truck in the courtyard, its

engine running. The boxes, split in places and lashed together with thick paper twine, leap in great arcs from man to man. They pass by a table, at which the little archivist touches and looks at them one last time; it is evidently difficult for him to part with them. He is grey, half the size of the soldiers, the inadequate back of head replaced by a tonsure the size of an old thaler coin. The boxes burst before him with a crash, dust flying into his nostrils. Sometimes one falls on his foot, apparently by accident. He coughs constantly, dabbing at his forehead with his handkerchief; his eyes trail after one box beneath his horn-rimmed spectacles, reaching out with his hands, calling out in a choked, high-pitched voice. In vain: the requisition process cannot be stopped. Refoulés – indésirables – inconnus – "homeless" – Arméniens. Soon he gives up untying the string; he has already broken two nails. One box harries the next – one-two, thud, thump; then the pace slackens, the human chain breaking off, as the pile topples over. Some of the soldiers start to sing; two of them chat across others in the line. One lights up a cigarette, just as a box comes flying towards his stomach; he has enough presence of mind to deflect it with a kick of his boot, without lowering the lighter from his face. "Goal!" Papers fly noisily in all directions. Bloody hell. We've got to scrabble around and pick all this lot up now... Christ, who's done one? You got a dead bird in your pocket or something? Outside, underneath the archway, the roar of engines, beeping horns, rises and falls; a van is hosed down. – Of an evening, one might come across Lieutenant S., with his pipe and slippers, an enormous torch tucked in his trousers. He picks odd papers up off the ground, blowing off the dust and sand, and peruses them, puffing away. Sometimes he folds something up, four times, eight times, and tucks it in his pocket. In the garden, blackbirds call, the stomp of a sentry on gravel...

International crisis at the knocking-shop

The tinned fish from the Soviet embassy was not actually that bad. It was probably sturgeon; at least, the tins featured a picture of a long, stiff fish, with a slightly raised snout. They had sent the stuff off to be opened in the *office*, along with quarter of a pound of tea, a shiny yellow bag which also stemmed from among the items seized at the Russian embassy. It was now steaming in the cups, a sepia-like browny-black; it tasted a bit oily, but was much stronger than the tea latterly on offer at the hotel, supplies of which were reputedly dwindling. There had not been any actual tea leaves in it, just sweepings, ground-up powder. Persian tea, Fräulein Klauter had claimed. – At dinner, talk had been of the article which had appeared in the evening edition of "Je suis partout", with a load of photos in which one could not see anything apart from a couple of faces, bleached white by the flash. And the raid at the Soviet embassy, which was carried out yesterday, including horror stories of trap doors, dungeons, electric vats for burning body parts which had been found, and which provided an immediate answer to a whole series of unexplained occurrences from recent years. However, the embassy staff could not be led to believe the one about the vats: they were simply a device for destroying files. They should have tried harder with the food. It was too late now. Alex, the driver – his mother was from Alsace, his father a Russian general, and he had lived in Spain for many years – had escaped with a whole briefcaseful. "Gentlemen," he had smirked, "this is the first and last time we get anything from Russia. There won't be much else out of them." He snapped his nicotine-stained fingers. "You can bet your life on it. Furs, caviar. This is not the French we're talking about here… There'll be nothing. Absolutely nothing." A completely impenetrable character, that Alex; beggars belief that someone like him was working for the German embassy. Also, he looked like an orangutan. He could pick up a chair with his teeth.

When they had finished eating, they listened to a bit of radio, on the set borrowed from the guardroom. But they couldn't get any dance music, and all the other stations only had German news in French, interspersed with lottery draws. It was so hot again today. And still no sign of it getting any cooler, even though it was already late into the evening. The tea made his shirt stick to his back again, just like at lunchtime when he fell asleep over that ring binder. Zitsche went over to the window and pushed open the shutters. It was still as bright as day. To the west, the sky was almost white, streaked with a couple of threadlike clouds from below; whiter than glowing wicks: one could hardly look at them. He was hit by a bludgeoning, monolithic heat. "Hey, quick, Rosy's back.

Damn, she's gone again." The girl in the short silk dressing gown who, in the evenings since the heatwave started, sometimes used to come out onto the balcony for a few minutes, the narrow, dusty railed ledge which ran along the length of the building. Probably still at school, a bit undeveloped. Someone once looked down her dress; there was hardly anything to see. They often used to watch her through the slats of the persiennes; if they opened them (the old things squeaked something chronic) she would disappear into the room in a matter of seconds. The balcony was empty again now; the door into the apartment stood open, but satin curtains, which hung down like sheets of iron, obscured the view. The piano started up: finger exercises the whole length of the keyboard, a laborious climb which often ended up running out of steam. An ancient old joanna, seemingly; it sounded like the strings had dried out, with no felt on the hammers. – Otherwise, they only knew the crazy old bird opposite with the mass of white hair, who used to grope around her great apartment the whole day half-naked with the windows wide open, calling for her cat. – It seemed to be getting even brighter outside, that furnace of a sky never letting dusk fall. One no longer noticed that the bedside lamp was still on; only the yellowy reflection on the sheets – the bed had already been turned down – reminded you of the fact. An illustrated magazine poked out from under the pillow, probably a copy of "Magazin". No, "Par le trou de la serrure", it was called. Indecent photos, yes, but in a quirky way. For instance, there was a woman, seen from behind, with nothing on apart from some little lederhosen, with large cut-out ovals over the buttocks. On the next page, the same woman, quite fat, with nothing on down below, but wearing a black silk bodice or something, laced across the back. Yawning, he tossed the magazine aside. "Right, Zitsche. I'm off. Time to hit the sack. I was going to have a bath, too, and write home…" Zitsche had been rummaging around, hunched, for some time in the bottom of his wardrobe, constantly battling with the door which, however far he pushed it back, kept silently swinging back and hitting him on the hip. Finally, he finished what he was doing, his head emerging out of the wardrobe a deep red and running with sweat. "Are we going for a fuck tonight or what?" He was almost bellowing. What was the matter with him all of a sudden? But why not? They hadn't mentioned it before. 200, 300 francs – he had been planning on still buying those brown-and-white summer shoes this month. But it was a possibility. "All right. If you [Sie] just wait one moment, I'll pop and get my hat."

Silly, them still calling each other Sie.* But that was Zitsche all over. Like at the Deligny pool yesterday, which was heaving again. He would rather wait around for half an hour on the slippery wooden planks, constantly being jostled by little sods and getting splashed by people alongside jumping into the water, than go into a cubicle with somebody else. In the end, he suddenly slipped away with not so much as a peep. When he was annoyed, one could only tell from behind: he would sweat behind the ears, which themselves appeared

---

* The formal form for "you" in German, like vous in French.

to be larger and more angular than usual. Yes, he had a handle on it, no two ways about it. His telephone manner was a complete disaster, so cold and off-putting, like a dog's nose; one could have given him a good slapping. He let you know it, too, that his intention had originally been a senior diplomatic career. And those couple of semesters he'd sat out doing law somewhere were always being rubbed in your face. It was only because all the girls even possibly worth considering were already taken. What it came down to was needing somebody to have a drink with and pour his heart out to of an evening. There was only Klauter left: her figure wasn't too bad, but that blotchy skin, and then there was that huge scar on her chin. She'd be up for it, though, according to Maxe, at least. He had gone to her room once to have a button sewn on his coat. He read a magazine. Suddenly, he heard behind him: "Please, please: I can't take it any more." The lovely creature was lying on the settee in her pyjamas.

On the way back from his room, he could feel something in his jacket, a lump in the breast pocket. Money, his pass, everything there. Damn it, he still had those half-dozen letters to post. To Monsieur le général So-and-so, and Monsieur le marquis and le conseiller départemental. Completely plain envelopes, no mention of the German embassy on them. – The door to Zitsche's room was open, the telephone jingling inside. Huh. Where's he got to? He's got a way with him… Must be in one of his moods again, the dog-day sulks… But wasn't that his voice in the room opposite? Sounds like all kinds going on, shrieking, all hell let loose; now they're in the bathroom… And that stupid whirring noise up by the ceiling... Oh, it was the woman with the parrot, the new typist at consular services, whose name sounds like an apple: Boskop, Drosskop, something like that. The telephone again. They're going to have ringing in their ears at this rate. Or maybe he should answer it. "Zitsche's phone... Hello? His Excellency can't come to the phone right now... Terribly sorry... he's just this minute left for Bad Boskop..." Oh well. I'll go without him. He had to go out anyway, on account of the letters. And no bugger could sleep in this heat.

At Solférino station he took the stairs down to the Métro. One could hardly make out the golden face of the clock on the War Ministry – darkness had finally come, all of a sudden, not from the sky but as if it had been exuded out of the walls, an infinitely fine, warm dust. From the very pores of the stones... There was a breeze on the stairs, hard to say if cool or warm and damp. What was that strange stumbling hoof noise at the end of the boulevard? Garde mobile, firemen's helmets with swishing tails? They'd better make sure they don't get stuck; the asphalt was literally melting in the heat at lunchtime today.

Probably best to get off at Trinité. Just not Pigalle: he had had enough of that lately, mille fois merci! The marks from his nosebleed still hadn't quite come out... The way that little toad in the red jacket, sitting at the back on the sofa with the three squaddies, suddenly pointed at him: "GFP!"* He had stood at the counter full of composure. Then he spilt his beer down his suit, a jet of hot steam shot out of

---

* *Geheime Feldpolizei*, the secret military police.

the coffee machine, the whole room swathed in mist, and he darted out the swing door, whirling into the street… Well, it was almost curfew, fortunately. Until then, he could walk a bit slower, till the soldiery had well and truly quit the field. Until midnight, when the officers started trundling in, it was peaceful, the tide recedes on the stairs, just the femmes de chambre clambering about with bed linen. The girls used to get changed, silk kimonos in green and pink in place of the sturdy little smocks they used to wear for the squaddies, petite silver slippers with swansdown. The streets already empty, with access restricted to those with a pass, the occasional figure touting for business or some such vagabond the only ones about; the hour of the German civilian!

A pass check right by the exit. He slipped the postcard with the Heidelberg Tun on it into the cellophane sleeve. The flics saluted while looking to one side. "Copain? Drôle de collègue?" But why did one of them snort, the one with the bulging nostrils? Give him a good stare. Then he came prancing up. "Monsieur désire quelque chose?" There was a real posse of policemen around the church. Three of them came down the Rue Blanche, one after the other, on bikes; they almost hit him. The last one, with the squeaky pedal brake, shining his light on the house numbers as he goes past. And now two motorbikes with sidecars, a man in each, roar up, banging and farting, from the Gare Saint-Lazare, rattling the windows all along the street. For a moment, one could see the glint of their helmets, but were they German army helmets or those worn by the French traffic police? In any event, the police were on their toes, in case the locals tried to kick up a stink over the Russia business. The Sûreté, anyway; large-scale. "The perfect mechanism" was how the detective superintendent recently expressed it. "Even we can learn a thing or two there." It seems there had been a demonstration yesterday in Vincennes, everywhere swarming with people: Zitsche had run into it in his car; they had gone swimming in the Marne. He spun the wheel and drove, full throttle, into the first side street, so he said. The French girl they had with them – her husband, an officer in the air force, was being held in Germany; she was working for some kind of repatriation committee; the embassy had officially sanctioned Zitsche associating with her – had had a screaming fit. Zitsche immediately phoned the réception at the Kommandatur. "Why hadn't he slapped her with a wet towel?" came the reply.

It was dark now – complete and utter darkness. A few steps away it merged into a solid mass, hot, thick; no breeze could get through. It would have been better to have changed his shirt quickly or at least freshened up his underarms. His solution: a quick tip of the old cologne bottle, give it a bit of a shake – an extremely thrifty procedure. "A fresh aroma, nice and clean." It was particularly oppressive here in the Rue Clichy. Not a bugger to be seen; the rubber soles of his shoes made a squelching sound as they scurried along. Ahead of him, there were only some of those clattering wooden sandals, hurrying home, but with a slight limp, so that he could easily have caught the woman up. But he didn't feel like it. She was bound to chat him up, and you couldn't see a thing in the pitch black. – A blue light was burning

at the entrance to "Shéherézade", caught by the peak of
the night porter's cap and the curved roofs of a couple of
limousines. – What was that dark groaning heap of rags in
the porch there? A pair of scrawny legs in bright stockings
poking out, obstructing the pavement. Evidently plastered,
the poor cow. Muttering to herself, too: "Ah – les salauds –
les salauds…" And the unmistakable smell of sick. Utter
disgrace – but it was no surprise. You will get drunk on only
two glasses if you've nothing lining your stomach. Anyway,
enough of the false pity! There hadn't been problems with
food in Paris for ages; you could still get everything round
the back: the city could get by like that for years. There was
no comparison with what Germany had to go through in
1917, '18! Time to get that straight. The bread had [blank] for
fourteen days, mind you; constant stomach cramps. There
was something funny with his rear end again. Maybe it was
those Bolshie fish products. The issue over the iron filings
in the chocolate had been cleared up at least. Essentially, he
hadn't been right since Sunday, when they got going on all
that Russian stuff. He'd been in bed till late morning, the
waiter informed him when he brought his meal to the room –
breakfast and lunch at all once. Then Zitsche had called. "You
watch: we'll all have to muck in now." That was nonsense;
there was no question of that. Whoever was claimed by the
Foreign Office was safe. After all, one had a job to do. They
couldn't send any old person here; foreign policy couldn't
be allowed to grind to a halt. That had been the problem in
the last war. It was quite understandable that the squaddies
were peeved when you stood next to them in the Métro

and they recognized you as a fellow German. It was one of those inevitable hardships. One assumed a statesmanly face and stared imperviously into the distance. And even if you really were called up, there would be training first; by the time you were finished, the war in the east would be well and truly over. News had come in today: things were going very well, though they couldn't give details. The fall of Moscow, Bümke, the legation councillor, had implied, anyway, was only a matter of days. And, crucially, encirclement operations, the famous pincer movement, had already resulted in huge successes. "There is no such thing as retreat à la 1812. It's all over, gentlemen…" – – It was a funny idea, actually, going to a whorehouse on one's own, and in this heat. You come across as a lecher, depraved, hurrying along the dark streets. It's all Zitsche's fault!

The glass door opened before he had even put his hand out for the bell-push. Strange. You usually have to ring for ages. Why's it so quiet? What's with all the candles? Where is everybody? What's going on? The chandelier hovered brightly up above, free from the usual smoke; the purring fan was an improvement, too. On the sofa, which in the past he had seen as many as eight squaddies squashed onto, lay a solitary green Tyrolean hat. A moment later and a man in shirtsleeves, wearing horn-rimmed spectacles, appeared, his bald pate streaming with sweat, like a projectionist in a cinema, a scene-shifter… Silently, as if she were trying to be self-effacing, with no arse to her, the reception girl slipped out into the little salon in front of him, like it was a house of mourning. Perhaps a court martial official was lying in state somewhere, struck down by a stroke while carrying out his duties... There was a crackling from the loudspeaker, like gravel being ground up, and the heat hit you like a club.

But then, in a black silk dress with a white insert, came the head of reception, the gouvernante, fluent German, a woman of stature. With a fan and a sopping wet handkerchief screwed up in her hand, quite out of puff. "But mon dieu, good evening, what's going on here? Good heavens..."

"Why? Should anything be the matter?"

"Where are your friends, et messieurs les soldats? Tous partis, mon dieu..."

"Avec cette chaleur, Madame..."

"Don't say that, monsieur. All the soldiers have gone to Russia; two divisions left Paris on the train last night."

"But that's not due to hap— Nonsense. Who comes up with this stuff? Je vous assure, Madame..."

"Encore deux jours comme ça, et je dois congédier ces dames. Nous mêmes, la direction va nous foutre dehors."... She pounds the crumpled handkerchief against her forehead, the fan whirling in front of her bust. "They say there have been significant losses on the German side. Quelle horreur cette guerre de Russie! Is that what you've heard, too?"

"Quite the contrary, Madame. Il faut garder votre sang froid, je vous en prie. Any German losses are quite disproportionate to the overall historical magnitude of our achievements..."

"Vous dites...? Where do you work, anyway? You get news...?"

"If anyone gets precise information, it's us. The emb—"
Holy shit, he almost gave the game away. Reveal himself as
a member of the embassy staff? He must be mad. There he
goes again with his childlike honesty, good old Honest Fritz
at a time when one should be on one's mettle; he really must
stop doing that. She certainly knew how to pump you for
information, this one: dignified, a lady of honour in her silky
attire, who ostensibly didn't know the difference between
regular army fatigues and the Luftwaffe. A silver cross hung
around her neck, at the entrance point to that stately bosom.
Divisions, losses... And how they'd impressed upon them
that places of amusement like this were playgrounds for the
foreign news service.

The Alsatian girl brought champagne, though he had
not ordered any. He could not bear her: the lascivious looks
from those keen, dark eyes; such an importunate, tactless
bitch. She even pushed his hand aside and sat on the arm
of the chair. Listen, kid: less of the free and easy. Either
you're here to receive guests and we pass the time of day,
a grown woman in an unfortunate situation and a young
man with political nous, or you're one of the staff and you
wait until you're called. We observe the proprieties, do you
understand? We're not in that much of a hurry; we're not
squaddies, who snaffle every morsel. – He had not forgotten
what she had said to his face in front of the whole crowd:
he didn't look German, she said. She should have kept quiet
about her ash-blond hair being out of a bottle; you could
see that a mile off...

"You still here? Not soldier? You job ver' important?"

The miserable trout. She could do with a good daily hiding. Just don't pay any attention... Cigarette? The woman in charge had sat down opposite, taking a sip of champagne. But then she was on her feet again, sighing: "Alors, je vais appeler ces dames."

Yes, indeed: appelle away. After all, I didn't come here to spend the whole night chatting. – The churr of a bell in another room, a clap of hands. Hopefully, the choice will be a bit better this time, something refined for once, something that usually the officers... Then the first one came in. He'd never had the honour: tall, in a pink tunic, thick golden-blond hair, a bit of all right; the perfect choice, really, but let's see the others first. The second one a bit too slick, with a scathing expression, but a wonderful arse. That's right, pull your robe a bit tighter; maybe a bit too full in the chest. Please, do come in! The little Annamese girl, collarbones protrude a bit, and those dull yellow doglike eyes, and that frizzy hair; Zitsche probably had her once. You can wipe that toothy grin off your face. Calm down: I'm not looking for anything exotic tonight; fuller, silent types are what I'm after... Then three come in at once, thrusting their way through the door, all in different greens, but all too gaunt, ungainly somehow, and their faces so long, like they were suppressing a yawn... Stop, sto-o-op, close the door, s'il vous plaît. That'll do for the time being; you can't get an overall view. It was all getting a bit much, what with the heat and the confined space. And it was so quiet, no whispering, giggling, just the rustle of silk and the gentle squeak of sandals. None of them looked at him either; their gaze was oddly angled up at the wall, with large drifting eyes, or pointed down towards the silver tips of their toes. One opened her kimono. Her listless breasts stared out in different directions, her navel a twisted mouth. What was the matter? None of them was quite there, as if in a semiconscious state, under chloroform. Their smiles looked like they had been badly painted on and then run, or drawn in saliva which had then dried out, a certain tautness, a forgotten boo-boo on the cheek. As if they had spent the whole day sleeping alternately with snowmen and stokers; or had Madame postponed their *dîner*, in view of the lack of clients? Water too hot? Spent the whole afternoon lying in the bath, playing with each other?

And still they poured in. There was already a second row before a third silently drew up behind, at an unbelievable rate. Who was that ancient battleaxe at the back with a face like some hideous mask? They were having a laugh, mobilizing both the back-up reserve and the home guard. He would have put the entire workforce at twelve women tops, but now there were twenty-five of them, thirty. Madame! Madame la sous-maîtresse! C'est trop! C'est pas correct! The next ones to arrive, the entire back of the room being full, lined up in front of the first row (pay attention, everyone! group shot), sprawling out... He could reach out a hand, but everything was swimming, bathed in a different light, as if behind ever-expanding heated glass, in a tropical aquarium. The door was now closed from outside. He sipped some champagne – it tasted like warm feet gone numb – opening his mouth a couple of times, but nothing came out. Don't scratch your head like that; it makes the whole room crackle.

Decisions, decisions… Hercules at the crossroads. He got out of it OK; he only had three to contend with.* And anyway, it all took place in the open air; he could scarper at any point. But for Erich (decisions, decisions…) at the fanny market, the dog-day duress, relentlessly staring the incalculable repercussions of the new military order in the face… – Find a few words, a joke, to burst the bubble of the whole sweltering charade… The supply outstripped demand. "Mesdames… L'offre surpasse…" What was demand? "Il me faudrait un certain recul… Je me sens mal disposé…" They appeared not to have understood. His words trailed around the room like the sound of creaking furniture. Their eyebrows only arched even more, their eyes drifting even further away, their shoulders slack and numb. But hello, right at the back, in the third row, that big, awkward mouth, with a golden twinkle in the corner: he recognized her from last time. She was the only one to sometimes look at him, too, the only one whose eyes actually had pupils – albeit withdrawn little eyes, like bedraggled grey mice. Certainly not classy. Rather on the contrary. But a nice bird, modest, made an effort, wasn't full of questions. But how to get her attention? Hesitantly, he raised half an arm in her direction – but another six would think he meant them. He couldn't remember their names… Yvonne, Yvette, Madeleine… But wait a minute.

---

* This short section conflates / confuses the parable of Hercules choosing between Vice and Virtue, and the Judgement of Paris (who had to choose between three goddesses: Hera, Athena and Aphrodite). The use of the name Erich here is perhaps a portmanteau of *er* and *ich*, the German for "he" and "I".

Seems the woman could read his mind... With a gentle *"pardon"*, narrow shoulders to the fore, she made her way through the ranks of her companions. And suddenly the whole nightmare was over, as if blown away. There was a silent swirl on the landing, those on the floor sprang up; all one saw was a couple of flapping sleeves, ends of belts, and the room, with its deep bluey-green carpet, was empty. Out on the stairs, they all suddenly started talking at once, like a school group, before it soon ebbed away again; there was no laughter. The girl came and sat on his knee. "Vous m'avez reconnue?" He had forgotten she had slightly bad breath. When he did not pull her towards him, she stood up again and busied herself with the champagne. He felt completely shattered, and his stomach felt funny again, like when he was outside. He didn't feel like it whatsoever; he hadn't wanted to all evening. And the girl didn't make any conversation, seemed completely inept. She probably had not been here long, a bit of a Cinderella; Madame had not wasted any time training her. Trust him to pick a dud. How embarrassing in front of the whole troupe. She must have felt pretty smug about it. Well, he'd soon knock that out of her. But he was mistaken there. And she asked him, in all innocence: "Vous ne voulez pas monter?"

The sous-maîtresse, whom they met on the stairs, looked at them wide-eyed. The whole floor lay in darkness, doors and windows open to let a bit of breeze through. The femme de chambre had to plunge into the darkness ahead of them, close the windows; then the light went on. The woman had caught his eye a number of times before: something angular about her face, a keen chin, but without compressing her lips. Something Slavonic about her. There was the suggestion of a limp, but it didn't matter; it made her bum stick out nicely. He tried to embrace her, while Madeleine (it was Madeleine) tucked the French letter under the pillow. But she slipped, sprang from his arms – impeccably practised hips – just said *"Pardon"*, as if they had accidentally bumped into each other; her face showed nothing. – A plethora of mirrors, the glaring sheets, and lamps, three, four; he immediately flicked off the lights on the ceiling, and the whole thing took on a much more intimate flavour. The women were still negotiating with each other; he heard something about "deux heures", then Madeleine pushed the bolt across before walking over: one-two, she had peeled everything off and was lying there. He usually kept his shirt on as he was a bit puny about the chest and shoulders, dreading comparisons with muscle-bound squaddies. It bothered him swimming, too. Zitsche had once passed the insinuating remark that the occupying powers' civilian forces should look just as strong and tough. But today everything was different. Deux heures: a ridiculously long time; other places allowed you scarcely half an hour and then hammered on the door before it was up. These ridiculous cufflinks. He had already stripped the shirt over his head, and now could not get it off his wrists, standing there shackled like an idiot. He felt strangely thin and white as he moved towards the bed, bringing a sudden touch of coolness with him, a delicate houseplant uncovered for the first time, touch-me-not nightshade; his feet sounded a different note, hot and loud. The girl seemed to sense it, too: Mais vous avez l'air d'une jeune fille, d'une petite jeune fille toute fraîche. Pourtant pas mal poilue – he had a good carpet of hair to his chest, quite out of keeping with the overall picture. – Things passed off without much ado, as if they had done it together a hundred times. He was glad he had managed it at all, as the woman did not interest him that much.

A couple in Montmartre

The steep, hot, stepped street leading down. One must take care on narrow steps in wretched hobnail boots, your toes pointing outwards, it makes your knees go funny. It would be better to take the steps sideways, like a steep slope. The girl is always a couple of steps below; she holds herself curiously erect, only her head hangs forward slightly, watching the tips of her shoes with downcast eyes. She is at least half a head taller than him [blank].

She must be a little tart. Maybe she's just having a day off today or something. She was off work, at any rate, when he chatted her up by that greengrocer's cart, where there are all those queues of women. A moment across the street, to ask after something in a shop, that skinny little barber leaning in the doorway, or to make a telephone call in the café on the corner. She wasn't quite properly made up either, far too much powder, with a kind of lilac tint to it, though her skin wasn't anything special, like that writing paper with a hammered finish, the more expensive kind. The lips painted hurriedly and much too large. Even the simple white blouse and the short dark skirt lent her a funny look of being off duty. That was why she had blinked in such surprise when he had accosted her, and kept looking back at him over her shoulder as they went along the street. But he was bloody glad to have found her. Was about to turn round again and go to the service club on Place Clichy for a proper cup of coffee, before heading back to barracks in good time: he had to be on duty again at ten o'clock. This funny old Montmartre (today was the first time he had been up here) did not impress him very much. An arduous business, cramped and airless. And dead somehow, a village at midday when folk are in the fields. But there weren't any fields any more, only the vast stone field of the city, from which this spurious, fake village had clambered up. No building over two storeys high, barns, sheds, immaculately rendered with a layer of mould. Sometimes it looked quite Sunday-like, as if, behind the closed shutters, everyone were taking an afternoon nap; greasy chimney walls, a wine-induced burp in a stairwell. Then there were windows with mangy brows, pairs of knickers hung up to dry, winking at you like the front of a town hall, or the Reichspost Hotel in Aschaffenburg. They stared at you like a blithering idiot blown in by the snow, some outlandish hooligan making an unholy row on the cobbles in his hobnail boots. But it was all a pose! Like some novice. There is no chance of an afternoon nap on an empty stomach. Wide awake, ears buzzing with ravenous hunger, wizened hags tickling the tops of their stoves. The smell of dried piss on hot bricks! And if the smell of cooking somewhere did then come wafting through, it was like the blast of a horn, loud and long, from a hot, wound coil of brass. It was quite a thing: it made one feel quite drunk, cast cats from the windowsills, made the birdcages seethe. But, before you knew it, the hot hunched cobblestones had snuffled it away. – There had been an attempt, here and there, at show, with half a tub of paint around a door, like a child with jam around its mouth; a scrap of coloured awning, a flower on a cactus. Sometimes, between two buildings, the sky dropped almost to the ground, only to be intercepted by a wall prickling with broken green glass. That dazzling white sky [blank], blazing just above your head. Or the occasional bruised notes of a barrel organ floating up from the city below, or – looking quite pathetic – a cabbage white from a nearby garden. It was already flagging [blank], spinning across the cobbles only inches from the ground. And sun everywhere! Shadows so thin one could scoop them up with a leg; there was barely any room for a shoulder. And sunburned ears peeling since yesterday. His neckcloth was already ripe for wringing out again. And the streets! The architect's pencil must have kept on breaking when he was drawing up the quarter, jogging the drawing board. Scraps of streets, entrails of hot stone, stillborn squares. And the people one saw, in the doorways, in the bars: lowlife that shunned the light, emaciated forms, loafing about astride wicker chairs, swilling out of toothglasses, and thinking insidious thoughts. There were hardly any girls about, only an adolescent creature now and then in clothes too big for her, a stick of bread under her arm or a net of onions, who only made eyes at you out of habit. It was far too early anyway, completely the wrong time of day. There had been some activity on one bleak little square: a muttering still hung in the trees, and a couple of thin, wispy notes from a violin; underneath the sunshades there sat a bunch of squaddies, aircrew mostly, with hunched backs, drawn-in necks, probably the odd girl among them. Sparrows and pigeons, and in the entranceways to the restaurants stood little violinists, dressed up as gypsies with silk sashes around their middles. He lost his way again after that. The north side of the hill. A patch of vineyard, here of all places. The view was down onto an entirely unfamiliar part of the city, which probably didn't have a real name, an out-of-the-way affair, a complete backwater. It wasn't worth committing to memory; it didn't want to be seen anyway. Gasometer after gasometer, and then that funny elongated church or airship hangar with the poisonous green roof. A cluster of trains crawling along, the front of each with a billowing yellowy-white mushroom of smoke. You couldn't make out where it all ended, as the horizon and the area leading up to it were steeped in a hot grey powdery haze.

Then he finally emerged onto the terrace outside the great white church, and the city lay spread out before him, cast wide, rolling out to the very edges of the world. Like a huge flat stone cake, floating in a milky cloud. One had to see it, of course. But once was enough: he felt quite queasy. From behind, that mountain of white marble weighing heavy on your shoulders; ahead, that impossible, inhuman sea of roofs wrenching at your guts. He really felt like he had done something wrong. At one point he had to rub the two lumps on the back of his head, which ordinarily he was only aware of when he had his helmet on; he should have them planed off, the company storeman had opined. It was within one's grasp – please, help yourself – and yet at the same time it seemed off limits. The inaccessible other side, not for people to see. If need be, one could view it through a keyhole, or build up a picture bit by bit through binoculars. But not with the naked eye, without some means of assistance: it was strictly forbidden to see cities warts and all. That was something for those stuffed shirts in the air force, the toffee-nosed soldiers, big-mouthed milksops like that one lieutenant on the advance here who had made himself a bed out of maps! He had always been drunk, too, whenever he had visited observation towers and the like with the unit. The womenfolk kept hold of their skirts, looking down at their chests rather than at the view, while a gentleman expounded on something from a book. One night, on the terrace above the Neckar,* the city twinkling with a thousand lights and as the moon was going down, he had had a painful urge in his rear, just as the moon was dropping behind the hill, the stars jangling louder and louder. He had leapt onto the wall, trousers down, and relieved himself over that city of light, the nightingales in the bushes singing out: "Show the world and all our foes, always ready primed to go!"† An

---

* A major tributary of the Rhine which passes through, among other places, Heidelberg, where Hartlaub went to university.

† Lyrics to a Nazi song.

older couple had remonstrated, and he had legged it, with old Max Scheurer, through a garden, crashing into a cold frame full of huge pale pumpkins. A sea of people was backing up at the bottom of the hill – noise filled his ears, but it was as if behind glass, drumming on a pane of glass. The tiny figures moved slowly off into the couple of streets one could see. And, rising up everywhere, there was this thin veil of dust and smoke, like the whole thing were part of some thousand-year combustion process, of limestone fermenting. Two squaddies had been standing there, one with his bootstrap hanging out, both wearing glasses, jabbing about with their arms and calling to one another when they had pinned something down, the such-and-such church, thingummy station. Stupid idiots. It was impossible to make anything out; better it should all stay clumped together, one thing inside another. If he wanted, he could put names to a couple of places. That half violin case, for example, floating far away to the right, was the Opéra, but that wasn't actually where it should be. And everywhere there were flashes of river, where they didn't belong.

Appendix

Sketches from Paris

'Two nuns drag a heavy sack between them…'

Chapelle Saint-Louis de la Salpêtrière

'Only the steep slate roof, straight and unbroken, and the gable end of the transept rise up over the cluster of tall, thin houses along the embankment...'

'The chestnuts have been cut back, beneath protruding corniced tops, into a thin, almost transparent wall…'

'The steamer has a boat in tow, the back of which lies deep in the water under the weight of three motionless French policemen.'

'...their caps, with deep furrows and pointed ends...'

'The two sphinxes, mounted on low plinths parallel to the main building, appear to have been made from the same stone. Painfully, with almost no necks, they raise their heads to the vertical…'

*'On the empty terrace, in the first row of tables, a sleeping
clochard, his bags on the chairs alongside. His head is
sunk forward, into the gaping neck of his coat.'*

*'The heavy tray clamped at shoulder height, head tucked
at an angle. The other hand is for opening doors. The long
coat-tails like the wing-cases of giant beetles…'*

'She is at least half a head taller than him…'